BAGUI

WYTHENSHAWE

HOSPITALS

A History

by

**Robert Price Davies
MD FRCS**

Bob Davies

2002

ISBN 0 9543392 0 7

Compiled, Typed and Designed by: Mavis and William Keith Plant

Printed in England by MFP Design & Print,
Longford Trading Estate,
Thomas Street, Stretford, Manchester M30 0JT

First Published 2002

Front cover photograph - Baguley Sanatorium patients having fresh air treatment

All profits from the sale of this book will be distributed equally to the North West New Heart - New Start Appeal Charity No.1049067 and the Neil Cliffe Cancer Care Centre, St Ann's Hospice Charity No. 258085.

Contents

Robert Price Davies
BSc MD FRCS Consultant Surgeon
Wythenshawe Hospital

ROBERT PRICE DAVIES, after National Service 1948-50, qualified MB ChB in 1958, having previously obtained a BSc in 1953. After pre-registration posts at Manchester Royal Infirmary in 1958-59, he had a year as demonstrator in anatomy at the University of Manchester. In 1960, he was awarded a Geigy Research Scholarship at Manchester Royal Infirmary and was awarded an MD. After registrar posts at Preston Royal Infirmary and Manchester Royal Infirmary, he went to Bristol Royal Infirmary and Bristol Children's Hospital as lecturer in surgery.

He returned to Manchester Royal Infirmary and Crumpsall Hospital as a senior registrar and in 1968 was appointed as consultant general surgeon at Wythenshawe Hospital where he remained for 24 years.

DEDICATION

I have written this book in tribute to the many thousands of patients who have attended Baguley Sanatorium and its successor, Wythenshawe Hospital.

Since October 1902, these patients have been cared for by many dedicated medical, nursing and ancillary staff who have seen the hospital grow in stature to the national reputation that Wythenshawe Hospital has today.

There are so many human stories - some happy, some sad - from the past century of medical care at Wythenshawe; one cannot record them all.

ACKNOWLEDGMENTS

In writing this book, I am indebted to all the patients of Baguley Sanatorium and Wythenshawe Hospital and to friends and colleagues who have contributed and supplied information. In particular, I wish to thank Mr John Dark, Dr Leslie Doyle, Dr Kathleen Lodge, Dr Clifford Franklin, Dr Desmond Pengelly, Mr Malcolm Towers, Mr Peter Hadfield and Mrs Ann Doolan.

I would like to thank Professor David Harnden, Chairman of South Manchester University Hospitals NHS Trust (SMUHT) for his help and support.

I am grateful to Professor John V Pickstone and the Northern Civic Society for allowing me to reproduce the early history of the Baguley site and Baguley Sanatorium.

A special debt is owed to Dr Peggy Arnell, Head of Research and Development at SMUHT, for advice and editing; also to Ms Helen Kitchen for help with designs.

I particularly want to thank Mavis and Keith Plant who have played the major part in the preparation of this book and whose contribution has been invaluable.

Thanks are also due to the John Rylands University Library of Manchester for permission to reproduce copies of photographs relating to the Out-patients Department of the Manchester Hospital for Consumption and Diseases of the Throat and Chest.

Certain information has been extracted from the records deposited in the Cheshire County Record Office, Duke Street, Chester and is reproduced with the permission of Cheshire County Council.

Some information contained in this book relating to St Anne's, Bowdon, was taken from *Records of St Anne's* written by Heather Jane Dentith.

The photograph of Princess Margaret at the opening of the new hospital has been reproduced with the permission of Manchester Evening News.

Finally I would like to thank all the patients who have contributed to the production of this book.

FOREWARD
by
The Rt Hon The Lord Morris of Manchester PC AO QSO

The tubercular poor was how Manchester's poorest of the poor often used to be described. My father, a disabled ex-serviceman, who died when he was forty-three, was one of them; I knew when I was a child exactly what tuberculosis meant.

Widely seen as a deficiency disease, it was a mass killer that met its match only when streptomycin was discovered. But long before then, caring for its victims was a life-long dedication for some of this country's finest-ever hospital staffs.

Baguley Sanatorium opened its doors a century ago for the treatment of patients with tuberculosis and its work was held in high regard and admiration as a haven of mercy far beyond Manchester and the North West.

The story of the sanatorium is told in these pages by a doctor - Robert Price Davies - no one more qualified to have done so. His timely and important book traces the development of one of the most advanced of Britain's contemporary hospitals - Wythenshawe - back to Baguley Sanatorium.

It was my great good fortune to represent Wythenshawe in the House of Commons for thirty-three years from 1964-1997. For twenty-four of those years, Robert Davies was a consultant general surgeon of renown at Wythenshawe Hospital. His patients were mostly my constituents and I heard at first hand of his abiding concern and commitment in always doing all that he could to help them.

His book deserves a wide readership and all possible success.

This was the award-winning design in a 1982 staff competition for a new logo for Wythenshawe Hospital. The designer, Miss Dilys Matthews, Superintendent Radiographer, explained her inspiration for the crest:

"As the catchment area for our patients covers such a wide area - from all points of the compass in fact, and as the name 'Wythenshawe Hospital' contains the four major compass point letters, this dictated the positioning of the name in the border. The caduceus, (snake entwining staff) being traditionally a symbol of health, points North and South. The wavy band, denoting the Mill Brook traversing the grounds of the hospital, points East and West. Wishing to demonstrate the long association with Baguley - the area and the hospital, the first quarter shows part of the Baguleys of Baguley crest. In the second quarter part of the Tattons of Wythenshawe crest. In the third and fourth quarters are symbols of the hospital's association with Lancashire and Cheshire respectively."

Chronicle of Notable Events

1865   French physician, Villemin, suggests that tuberculosis is communicable disease.

1875   Manchester Hospital for Consumption and Disease of the Throat founded at 18 St. John Street, Manchester.

1880   Recognition that 'open-air' treatment was an effective cure for tuberculosis.

1882   The bacillus of tuberculosis isolated and identified by Robert Koch.

1884   St Anne's Home, Bowdon was founded.

1885   Out-patients clinic opened on Hardman Street, Manchester.

1890   Introduction of tuberculin as a possible cure.

1899   Launch in Manchester of notification scheme by Dr J Niven.

1900   Accommodation at St. Anne's Home, Bowdon expanded to fifty beds.

1901   Manchester Sanatorium opened at Delemere.

1902   Baguley Sanatorium for treatment of infectious diseases opened by Earl of Derby.

1911   National Insurance Act became Law.

1912   Baguley Sanatorium converted into tuberculous sanatorium with 150 beds and cases of other infectious diseases transferred to Monsall Hospital.

1914   Clinic on Hardman Street, Manchester adapted as the city's tuberculosis dispensary.

1922   Appointment of Dr Hugh Trayer as Medical Superintendent at Baguley Sanatorium.

1933   Combined chapel and recreation hall opened.

1939   Emergency Medical Hospital was built on Baguley site next to the older tuberculosis wards and became known as the 'hutted area A'.

1941   An operating theatre with six bed recovery unit opened.

1948   Start of the National Health Service.

1950   Last of military patients departed.

1952   Manchester Regional Board plans a general hospital with Baguley remaining a chest hospital.

1952   Hutted area became Wythenshawe Hospital.

1952	A new chest clinic opened at Wythenshawe Hospital.
1955	The Ministry of Health included Wythenshawe in a list of new hospitals to be opened.
1959	First open heart operation performed at Wythenshawe Hospital.
1959	Wythenshawe Sub-Committee of the Hospital Board decided to scrap previous plans to build a new hospital in the hutted area and proposed to build in the grounds of Baguley Hospital.
1961	Second phase of the new Wythenshawe Hospital included in building plans for 1964-5.
1963	Work started on the building of Maternity Unit in Wythenshawe Hospital complex.
1965	Maternity unit opened by Minister of Health, Mr Kenneth Robinson.
1969	Plastic surgery unit moved to Withington Hospital.
1973	The new hospital at Wythenshawe opened by Princess Margaret.
1987	First heart transplant carried out.
1994	Formation of South Manchester University Hospitals NHS Trust covering Withington and Wythenshawe Hospitals.
1994	Glaxo lung research unit built.
1994	Cardiac catheterisation laboratories opened.
1994	Bradbury Trust cystic fibrosis unit opened.
1994/5	Total of 51 heart transplants performed (23 heart transplants 5 heart and lung, 15 single lung and 8 double lung.)
1995	Day case facility (Baguley Suite) opened.
2000	Extension to Children's Unit opened.
2001	Education and research centre opened.
2001	Opening of new acute unit on completion of the first phase of £113 million development on Wythenshawe Hospital Site.

The Township of Baguley

The Domesday Survey of 1086 documents the area in which Baguley Sanatorium and the present Wythenshawe Hospital are built:

Gislebertus and Ranulfus and Hamo held Sunderland and Baggiley. Alweard and Sucga and Wudumann and Pat held it as 4 manors and were free men. There is 1 hide paying geld. There is land for 1¹/₂ ploughs. The whole is waste: In the time of Edward the Confessor it was worth 3s.

Gislebertus, Ranulfus and Hamo were all major land holders in Cheshire at that time - Gislebertus probably being Gilbert de Venables (*Baron of Kinderton)* who held 19 manors in Cheshire and 7 elsewhere; Ranulph as Masnilwarin (*supposed to be the ancestor of the Mainwarings*) who held 14 manors in Cheshire and 10 elsewhere, and Hamo de Massey (*Baron of Dunham Massey, Sunderland being located within the town of Dunham Massey*) who held 12 manors in Cheshire and 9 elsewhere.

Around the reign of King John (1199-1216), the then Lord of Dunham Massey, Hamon Massey, gave two parts of Baggiley to Matthew de Bromhalo. The township of Baguley gave name to the family of Baggileys who were seated there as early as 1234 when Willo de Baghel was a witness to a Toft Charter. It is possible that the change in ownership was as a result of a marriage settlement between the Masseys and the Baguleys.

Around 1320, Sir William Baggiley was granted Ryle Thorn and Alveley Hay by the de Stokeport family, and it was about this time that Baguley Hall was built.

The Hall, which is one of the earliest timber-framed houses in Cheshire, is a fine example of a medieval hall. It is built in the Viking house style of an upturned boat of heavy planks. The original Hall probably only consisted of the Great Hall and a passage on its northern side. The Hall was greatly extended between the fifteenth and nineteenth centuries with a northern wing added (later refaced in brick) and a wing to the south added during the Georgian period.

After many changes in ownership, the Hall became part of the Wythenshawe estate of the Tatton family, passing into the hands of Manchester Corporation when the estate was acquired for council houses in the middle of the twentieth Century.

Baguley Hall - 1919

In the early part of the fourteenth century, Sir William Baggiley's son, John Baggiley, made a gift of the manor of Baggiley and his manors of Hyde and Levenshulme to Sir John Legh of Knutsford, agreeing that Sir John should settle them on John Baggiley and his male heirs. The manor passed on the marriage of Isabel Baggiley in 1355 to a member of the Legh family. The manor remained in the Legh family until the Legh family died out in 1691, subsequently passing through the hands of the Allen, Jackson and Massey families before becoming part of the Tatton estate in the mid-eighteenth century. By the middle of the nineteenth century, the present layout of the area was becoming established, as can be seen on Bryant's 1831 map of the area.

The commercial directories of the period describe Baguley as a township and straggling village, with *Bagshaw's Directory* of 1850 containing the following details:

Baguley, township and straggling village, is situated about two miles E. by N. from Altrincham, and contains 1769 A. 2 R. 26 P. of land, of which 92 acres are comprised in Baguley moor. In 1841, there were 97 houses and 505 inhabitants. Population in 1801, 423; in 1831, 468. Rateable value, £2,106. Thomas

The Great Hall, Baguley Hall - 1826

William Tatton, Esq., is the principal landowner and lord of the manor, besides whom the executors of the late Robt. Baxter, Esq., are also proprietors, and there are several resident freeholders. A farm in this township has been purchased, to augment the living of Ringway Chapel. The manor, having been part of the barony of Dunham-Massey, became, at an early period, the property of the Baguleys, a co-heiress of which brought it in marriage to Sir William Legh, whose family continued proprietors till their line terminated in Edward Legh, who died in 1688. The manor was subsequently held by the Allen and Jackson families. The vicarial tithes are commuted for £34, and rectorial for £153.

Baguley Hall exhibits a fine specimen of the domestic architecture of olden times. It is composed of oak and wicker work, with bay windows. In the interior are some remains of oak work, elaborately carved. This was the ancient seat of the Baguleys. It is now converted into a farmhouse. Portions of the hall have been taken down at different periods. On Baguley Moor, 4 miles E.N.E. from Altrincham, which is near the hall, is a large tumulus. Dr. Gower, in a letter to the Rev. Mr Harwood, of Chester, on the authority of Dr. Piercy, says, that one of the Leghs, of Baguley, wrote several historical poems, in the reign of Henry VII. The manuscript is described to be in folio, entitled "Scottish Fielde." An annual sum of £5.5s., is received from Lord Stamford. The poor also participate in Houghton's Charity.

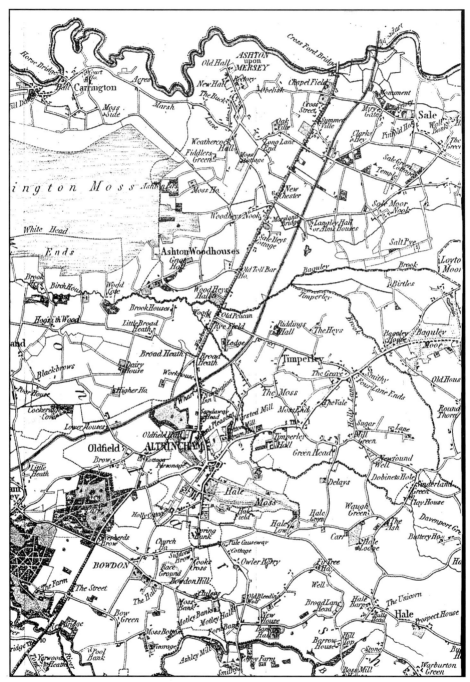

Bryant's map of 1831

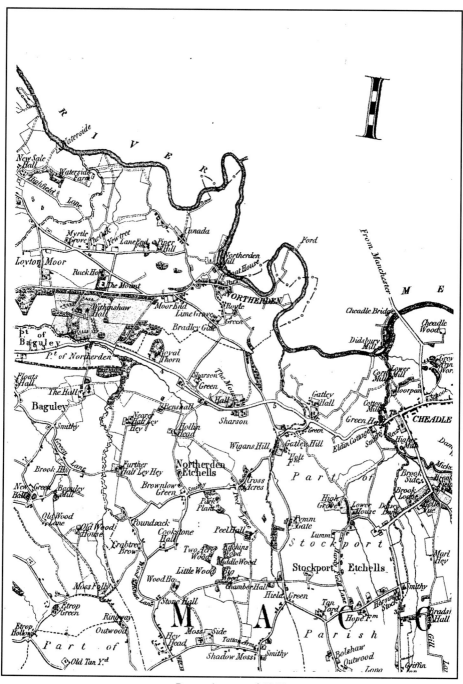

Bryant's map of 1831

5

At the time of the 1881 Census, the Hall was occupied by William Marsland who farmed 296 acres and employed 11 men. All the family had been born in Baguley and, on the night of the census, William and his wife, Frances, and seven children were living in the Hall. Attached to the Hall were some temporary cottages housing farm labourers, the majority of whom had been born in County Mayo, Ireland.

Towards the end of the nineteenth century, the Urban District Council of Withington - realising the need for a hospital for the treatment of infectious diseases - negotiated the purchase of 37 acres of land some nine miles from Manchester. The land was devoted for the most part to dairy farming and market gardening and was farmed by a Mr Lowe who owned the land and Baguley Lodge, then a thatched cottage. The land had previously been farmed by the Woods - Thomas and John Wood succeeding Mr W Helsby who owned the property in 1852 (the latter presumably being the son of Richard Helsby listed in the Tithe award of 1838).

The original meaning of Baguley is 'Badger clearing or wood'. It has been spelt in various forms over the years ranging from Bagelei (1086), Bageley (1210), Baggkeleg (1274), Bagguley (late 13th and early 14th centuries), Baglegh (1310), Bagelegh (1406), Baygulagh (1500), Bagele (1516), Bagalegh (1570) to Bageleigh in 1699, before settling down in its present form.

Wythenshawe Hall

Wythenshawe Hall and the estate have hosted many social events associated with Baguley and Wythenshawe Hospitals.

The Hall itself dates back to the Tudor period and possibly earlier. According to an ancient document, an earlier house had been destroyed by fire and rebuilt by Robert Tatton *circa* 1540 re-using timbers and other internal features from the earlier building.

Wythenshawe Hall

In 1642-43, the Hall was subjected to a siege by Cromwell's troops led by Colonel Robert Duckinfield. Robert Tatton, the owner of the Hall at that time, defended the Hall using Royalist soldiers drawn from the surrounding areas of Didsbury, Sharston and Baguley.

In 1926, the Hall passed to Manchester Corporation and the central portion became a museum. The first floor bedrooms behind the withdrawing room were converted into one large exhibition room, the Gillows bookcases in the library were turned into showcases and the former Servants Hall and outbuildings on the far side of the courtyard at the southern end of the house were rebuilt to serve light refreshments to visitors.

In the period 1947-52, a major programme of demolition and reconstruction was undertaken. The front facade of the South Wing, the Conservatory and the extension to the back staircase were demolished. The rendering on the central portion of the Hall, which had decayed behind the ivy planted *circa* 1839, was replaced with black and white timbering, although there was no historical evidence that the Hall had ever had a facade in this style.

A renewed outbreak of dry-rot and beetle infestation in 1978 closed the Hall until 1983 to enable treatment to take place. In 1985, the Library Wing was re-opened after extensive conservation work.

Origins of Hospitals Before 1948

Prior to 1948, there were two distinct types of hospitals in England and Wales which had evolved from quite different roots: the Voluntary Hospitals and the Municipal Hospitals.

Some of these hospitals date back to institutions founded in the Middle Ages by the Monastic Orders, but when the monasteries were dissolved during the reign of Henry VIII, most of the monastic foundations died out. There are still existing hospitals which are directly descended from religious foundations or monasteries such as St. Thomas's Hospital and St. Bartholomew's Hospital in London.

The voluntary hospitals were ordinarily charitable institutions for the sick poor which were founded and endowed by local citizens. Their medical staff were men who gave their services without charge to care for their less fortunate fellow-men who were sick. These hospitals were set up only where there were people with sufficient money and public spirit to found them. The great period for the foundation of the voluntary hospitals was the eighteenth and nineteenth centuries and most of the big London hospitals and a number of hospitals in the provinces were thus founded between 1720 and 1870. As the medical staff received no money for their work in the hospitals, they had to be sure of a sufficiently large private practice in the neighbourhood in order to earn a living. As time went on, people began to pay the hospitals what they could afford for their medical care, but they did not pay the specialists nor did the specialists receive any of the money paid to the hospitals by the patients. As a result, the unpaid medical staff still had to continue to work in localities where there were sufficient well-to-do people able to pay as private patients.

Over time private patient numbers declined, making it necessary for hospitals to start paying their medical staff. All the hospitals, with one or two exceptions, were non-profit making and relied for their finances partly on voluntary contributions, gifts and legacies, partly on what patients could afford to pay, and partly on contributory schemes which were a form of voluntary insurance against illness and hospital treatment. In addition to this, the statutory local authorities also paid certain sums to the hospitals for services rendered on their behalf. Manchester Royal Infirmary, for example, was a voluntary hospital, funded by subscribers and staffed by unpaid physicians attending poor patients nominated by subscribers.

Dispensaries were run in much the same way as voluntary hospitals - but without beds - and operated independently of the hospitals. They were designed for out-patients who could visit the dispensary or home-patients who were visited at their own homes. They came to be used for the treatment of fever epidemics which occurred on a regular basis through the eighteenth and nineteenth centuries and into the early part of the twentieth century. Finance for dispensaries generally came from leading industrialists and gentlemen of the area; for example, the industrialists and gentlemen of Ancoats and Ardwick gave one or two guineas per year to the dispensary.

Most infirmaries included infectious diseases, children and midwifery cases. By the end of the nineteenth century, most of the dispensaries had been converted into infirmaries or closed. At about this time, infirmaries were beginning to be called 'hospitals'. 'Cottage hospitals' became the preferred form of medical charity for small towns, usually organised by local practitioners who expected payment from their patients. Town infirmaries and cottage hospitals continued as independent voluntary associations until 1948.

The municipal hospitals grew up equally haphazardly from quite a different route, that is, the Poor Law hospitals. These derived from the old system of Poor Law Relief, established in the time of Queen Elizabeth I largely as a result of the dissolution of the monasteries and the loss of their organisations. These Poor Law institutions and workhouses grew up during the next three and a half centuries. They provided care for the destitute sick and the wards were frequently rather deplorable places.

During the second half of the nineteenth century, people became more interested in welfare work and, by the beginning of the twentieth century, these institutions began to improve. In 1930, the responsibility for administering the Poor Law institutions and workhouses was transferred from the Poor Law Board of Guardians to the County and County Borough Councils. They were given power, if they wished, to take over workhouse wards for the sick and run them as hospitals. Most of the wealthier and more progressive councils did this. Between 1929 and 1939, authorities such as London, Manchester, Birmingham and Middlesex took over the workhouse infirmaries and started to develop and staff them properly. Soon they were rivalling the voluntary hospitals. These new municipal hospitals usually had full-time salaried medical staff, and were governed by County and County Borough Council members. By the outbreak of the Second World War, 60 per cent of beds were in municipal hospitals.

Until 1938, the Ministry of Health had only been concerned with the municipal hospitals but, during wartime, it found itself having to supervise a comprehensive hospital service for the first time. The Emergency Hospital Service which came into being was extemporised on top of the existing organisation and left in the hands of the people running it at the time.

In 1943, a detailed survey of all the hospitals in the United Kingdom and their work was undertaken by teams of experts (some appointed by the Ministry of Health and others sponsored by the Nuffield Foundation). The resulting reports provided the basis for much of the country's subsequent hospital planning.

Causes and Early Treatment of Tuberculosis

Illness was, in large measure, caused by the conditions in which people lived: the damp cellars; cramped living with many people in close contact; the filthy undrained streets; the foul and contaminated air, and the miserable diet of the workers - particularly in the cities and large towns.

Working conditions did not help and, in many instances, were a direct cause of illness. In an article in the *North of England Medical and Surgical Journal* of 1831, JP Kay refers to the diet of cotton workers at that time:

The whole population employed in the various branches of the Cotton Trade, rise at five o'clock in the morning, work in the mills from six till eight o'clock, and return for half and hour or forty minutes to breakfast. This meal generally consists of tea or coffee, with a little bread. Oatmeal porridge is sometimes, but of late, rarely used and chiefly by the men, but the stimulus of tea is preferred and especially by the females. The operatives return to the mills and work shops until twelve o'clock when an hour is allowed for dinner. The dinner is greedily devoured. It generally consists of boiled potatoes. The mess of potatoes is put into one large dish, melted lard and butter are poured upon them, and generally a few pieces of fried fat bacon are mingled with them, and, but seldom, a little meat. The family sits round the table, and each rapidly appropriates his portion on a plate or, they all plunge their spoons into the dish, and with an animal eagerness, satisfy the cravings of their appetite. Some families provide a greater proportion of bacon or other animal food, but those who are most subject to gastralgia seldom taste flesh meat: and the quality consumed by the labouring class in general is not great. At the expiration of the hour they are all again employed in the work shops or mills, where they continue until seven o'clock or to a later hour, when they generally again indulge in the use of tea, often mingled with spirits, accompanied by a little bread. Oatmeal or potatoes are, however, taken by some a second time in the evening.

Kay suggested the following diet:

Three meals in the day - a breakfast consisting of milk or rice milk, and stale wheaten bread, at the usual hour - a dinner of a few ounces of animal food, and stale wheaten bread, without any vegetable - and in the evening, a supper of milk and bread.

However, there was one serious problem: Kay was discussing carders, spinners and weavers, few of whom could afford the diet suggested. Furthermore, the Ancoats dispensary in Manchester - unlike some other dispensaries - did not provide food.

In the *Artisans and Machinery Journal* of 1836, a surgeon, Peter Gaskell, referred to "the 'stunted, enfeebled and depraved' mill-workers, contrasting them with the rural population, who had hardly a day's illness. Here was the medical aspect of the country-town antitheses. In the country, life was vigorous and so was disease; death, when it came, was rapid. In the town, life was one long disease, and death the result of physical exhaustion."

For most people, consumption (tuberculosis) was a lingering illness - where one's condition worsened over months or years and almost certainly ended in death. Given the huge potential 'demand' for care and treatment and the impact of the disease on the public's health, consumption should have been an area of major medical activity. In fact, it was ignored at almost every level of medicine.

In some countries, tuberculosis acted like a veritable plague - so much so that, in the middle of the eighteenth century, tuberculous persons were treated as dangerously infectious. The severest measures of isolation and disinfection were taken in Italy, Spain and France, with laws passed in Italy and Spain to enforce stringent precautions.

It was, however, reserved for a French physician, Villemin, in 1865, to bring together the various facts indicating that the disease was communicable. By producing the disease in rabbits and guinea pigs by the inoculation of tuberculous matter, he was able to show that it could be conveyed from one animal to another. A French veterinary surgeon, Chauveau, demonstrated that the disease was conveyed to bovines by the ingestion of tuberculous material.

Throughout the whole of the nineteenth century and well into the twentieth, tuberculosis was the commonest and most lethal disease of the town-dwelling population. The figures, as revealed in the case-notes, are quite staggering. In many years, tuberculosis accounted for over a quarter of all in-patient admissions. The disease was incurable - yet a patient's past history of tuberculosis was generally ignored by doctors. Once diagnosed as tuberculous, the patient would not be re-admitted to hospital except in unrelated illness or accident. Surgery for tuberculosis accounted for over 20 per cent of all operations: removal of glands, the drainage of an abscess (the typical 'cold' abscess or the 'psoas abscess' derived from tuberculous infection of the spine) and the amputation of limbs for the classical 'white swelling' of scrofula which (although regarded as a separate entity) was caused by tuberculous infection of the joint.

Robert Koch was born in 1843 at Klausthal in Hanover. He graduated from Gottingen and, after serving in the Franco-Prussian war, settled as a kind of state-supported general practitioner in the country district of Wollstein. He had no proper laboratory and no special training but he was interested in the microscope and spent much of his spare time examining specimens.

Robert Koch who identified the tuberculosis bacillus in 1882

Koch is most widely remembered for isolating and identifying the tubercle bacillus which bears his name. In a 1882 paper, he described the organism as the cause of tuberculosis and laid down the rules of the relationship between bacteria and disease. Around 1890, he introduced tuberculin as a supposed cure. Had tuberculin proved successful, the story of surgery during the next fifty years would have been very different. In time, tuberculin came to be used as a 'patch test' - a local reaction showing whether or not the subject had been exposed to tuberculosis.

The possibility of using bacteriological diagnosis to detect early cases of tuberculosis was a considerable help to physicians interested in treating the disease. The ability to recognise the bacteria in the environment, especially in the dust of infected houses, helped confirm the previous statistical association between tuberculosis and dark, unventilated homes. The discovery that sunlight killed bacteria helped explain the value of open-air sanatoria, a system of treatment which had been extensively developed in Germany where the mortality from tuberculosis was even higher than in England.

What was novel about Koch's work was his absolute conviction in the contagiousness of tuberculosis. But this claim was largely ignored in Britain until the late 1890s. In 1885, a collective investigation by the British Medical Association found that only a quarter of doctors believed consumption to be truly contagious.

The 1880s saw the proliferation of treatments and advice on the avoidance of consumption. Until then, therapy had involved a range of symptomatic measures to control coughing, night sweats and tiredness, together with a judicious combination of sedative and tonic medicaments and measures to counter wasting. CJB Williams of the Brompton Hospital claimed that the introduction of cod-liver oil in the 1880s had brought about a therapeutic revolution by building up patients' strength. The most novel treatments were those which sought directly to destroy bacteria in the patient and were mostly techniques from antiseptic surgery. Means of delivering antiseptics to tubercular lesions included inhalation (by the use of masks soaked in carbolic and creosote), the direct introduction of antiseptics into the lungs by injection, and the intravenous injection of antiseptics in the hope that they would be carried to the lungs by the circulation.

Most notable was the new impetus given to 'climatic treatment' and its transformation into the 'open-air' or 'hygienic' treatment. A 'change of air' remained the preferred treatment throughout the 1880s and 1890s. An important part of the 'open-air' treatment became removal of the patient 'to an area free of the active virus', and the prevention of the 're-breathing' of infected air.

The 'cure' required a lengthy residence in an institution where the patient, under strict supervision, spent as much time as possible in the open air, took an ample and rich diet, and undertook rest or exercise as recommended. Patients' conditions were constantly monitored by thermometry, auscultation and bacterial examination of sputum. Sanatoria sought early or incipient cases where a patient's infectivity was low. (Advanced cases were avoided if possible: these were inevitably terminal and highly infectious. For these, isolation was seen to be appropriate, though few facilities were provided outside of the Poor Law.) The dynamics of the 'open-air' treatment - for example, the properties of the air or its mechanism of action - received no attention. There was mention of the disinfecting powers of ozone and sunlight; of changes in the depth and regularity of breathing; of the linings of the lungs being toughened, and of improved circulation, but none of these was seen to have any specific effect. What was said about the open air and outdoor life was that it provided a near-aseptic environment, and hence individual isolation, for each patient. Therapeutic action was usually attributed to dietary management, rest and exercise, hygienic training or medical treatment.

Not everybody supported the idea of sanatorium treatment. The provision of sanatoria for the working class was opposed on economic grounds, particularly the futility of helping people with weak constitutions and unhygienic habits who would return to conditions which had produced the disease in the first place.

Sanatorium treatment was based on a 24-hour timetable for each patient. The schedule went beyond medical routine and personal hygiene, to requirements for social activities and relationships and codes of behaviour. The problems of running a sanatorium full of mostly young patients, who were often not incapacitated and with time on their hands, are not difficult to imagine. Most sanatoria segregated male and female patients, though it was difficult to prevent mixing when not only the doors and windows were open but the walls too! Some patients were dismissed for disciplinary reasons and most found the regime harsh: sanatorium superintendents were often said to be autocrats or martinets.

In 1886, Dr James Niven was appointed Medical Officer of Health for Oldham. He believed that the facts were sufficient to support public health measures, but that any application of them must depend on an intimate knowledge of the mode and conditions of infection. He therefore visited a series of houses, in which deaths from tuberculosis had occurred, to investigate the conditions under which the infection had appeared. He made a statement on the subject in his first Annual Report in 1886. One of his findings was the absence of any history of human infection in many of the children who had died of the disease.

In 1890, he visited the houses at which a second series of deaths had occurred and, while the history of infection in cases of pulmonary tuberculosis was as striking as before, it seemed to him that healthy persons did not contract tuberculosis except after intimate and prolonged exposure to infection.

In the interval between these observations, Dr Niven was commissioned in 1890 by the Medical Society of Oldham to visit Berlin and report whether it was desirable to adopt the new tuberculin treatment being used there. He concluded that it was not, but he did see tuberculin as an excellent means of determining the presence of the disease in obscure cases, if used in very small doses.

Several of the British initiatives in the study and treatment of tuberculosis came from the Manchester district. From the mid-1880s and especially in the Edwardian period, there was considerable collaboration between University medical scientists, medical officers of health and clinicians working in the Manchester Hospital for Consumption and Diseases of the Throat and Chest. Sheridan Delépine, Professor of Pathology (later of Bacteriology) at the University of Manchester Medical School, was one of the country's leading bacteriologists and he was largely responsible for demonstrating the transmission of tuberculosis to man via the milk of infected cows.

JFW Tatham, Medical Officer of Health in Salford (1873-88) and Manchester (1888-93), demonstrated the need for better housing to combat tuberculosis. His successor in Manchester, James Niven, had already conducted investigations of the homes of phthisis sufferers in Oldham, and had almost persuaded Oldham Council to make tuberculosis a notifiable infectious disease. That plan, for which Niven had won the approval of Oldham medical practitioners, would have been the first such scheme in Britain.

Niven and others used the North Western Association of Medical Officers of Health to extend their campaign for notification. They were supported by the Manchester & Salford Sanitary Association. In 1899, Manchester Corporation agreed to the scheme and Niven drew up a comprehensive plan combining education, disinfection of the homes and hospital treatment in the hope of reducing the incidence and mortality of the disease. Manchester was second only to Brighton in introducing notification. Niven's plan was only partially realised, but it was an important step towards larger schemes which became possible in Manchester and elsewhere after the 1911 Insurance Act introduced benefit payments for the domiciliary and sanatorium care of tuberculosis patients.

Veranda off the Baguley Sanatorium wards which provided 'open-air' treatment

The Early Years

Tuberculosis is an infectious, communicable disease, caused by the bacterium *Mycobacteruim tuberculosis* and most frequently affecting the lungs. The disease is usually contracted by breathing in the bacterium or by swallowing contaminated food. Most commonly, the mode of spreading the disease is

Aerial view of Baguley Sanatorium - circa 1925

sneezing and coughing by an infected person.

Overcrowding and insanitary living conditions, particularly in the city areas, were the main contributing factors to the spread of the disease. In Victorian England, tuberculosis - especially pulmonary tuberculosis - was the major single cause of death. In the 1850s, tuberculosis accounted for about 12 per cent of the deaths in the Manchester area, but it was not a prominent disease in the records of the voluntary general hospitals. Few patients were admitted to the wards, because little could be done for them and the progress of the disease was so slow.

According to the *Decennial Supplement of the Register of General Reports*, 2,000 people a year died of tuberculosis in the Manchester conurbation during the 1870s. A high proportion of these cases must have been treated by Poor Law medical officers, and some would have been housed in Poor Law institutions. Around 1900, there were about 330 beds for tuberculosis patients in Manchester and Chorlton Poor Law hospitals.

Manchester was at the forefront of the fight against tuberculosis. At a meeting in February 1875 in Manchester Town Hall, Dr Shepherd Fletcher read a circular calling a public meeting to consider the desirability of establishing a hospital in Manchester for consumption and diseases of the throat.

At this meeting it was resolved:

1. That such a hospital be at once provided and opened as soon as possible, there being no other hospital for similar purposes in Manchester.

2. That WH Houldsworth Esq be appointed President of the hospital for the ensuing year.

3. That Messrs Seppoe, Bremner, Nicholls and Goldschmidt be appointed Vice Presidents of the hospital for the ensuing year.

4. That Charles Lings Esq be appointed Treasurer of the hospital for the ensuing year.

5. That Richard Hankinson Esq be appointed Honorary Secretary of the hospital for the ensuing year.

6. That Doctors Shepherd Fletcher and Alexander Hodgkinson be appointed Medical Officers of the hospital.

A later meeting on 22nd February 1875 resolved that:

1. Messrs Midgley Brothers, Chemists, St Ann's Square, Manchester, be hereby appointed Dispensers to the hospital.

2. The Manchester and Salford Bank be appointed Bankers to the hospital.

3.   Mr McKee be appointed the Collector and Mrs McKee the Matron of the hospital at a joint remuneration of 27/- per week, with coal, gas and one servant provided for them at the expense of the hospital. Mr McKee to receive, in addition to the above, remuneration and commission of 5 per cent on the sums collected by him.

It was further resolved at this meeting that the secretary and medical officers draw up and insert an advertisement in the Manchester newspapers announcing the formation of the hospital and appealing for public support, and, that 2000 copies of the appeal be printed and circulated amongst the public.

The rules for both IN and OUT patients were also finalised at this meeting including:

Swearing or the use of obscene language is strictly prohibited.

Patients are not allowed to remain out after 4 p.m. in winter and 8 p.m. in summer.

Subsequently, the Manchester Hospital for Consumption and Diseases of the Throat and Chest was founded by Dr Shepherd Fletcher and Dr Alexander Hodkinson, initially occupying a house at 18 St John Street with accommodation for eight in-patients.

In 1881, there were only 47 in-patients and 61 out-patients but, through the 1880s, support for the hospital grew as tuberculosis began to attract more public attention.

On Wednesday 12th July 1882, a special meeting was called by the committee to consider an offer made by Mr Joseph Sidebotham to sell his home 'The Beeches' in Bowdon for the sum of £5,000 to serve as the hospital, with a contribution of £500 towards the purchase.

Initially, the hospital committee felt that they could not afford his kind offer. However, 'The Beeches' was in an ideal location for the treatment of consumption, being in an airy healthy locality 10 miles south of the city. On 9th November 1883, Alex Hodgkinson, Arthur Ransome and H Young visited 'The Beeches' and reported:

'Gentlemen

We are of the opinion that the best site for a consumption hospital that has offered itself in this neighbourhood is Bowdon.

We are also unanimous is preferring a new hospital if it can be obtained.

We are unable to speak so decisively as to Hale but think it should be inspected.'

Prior to this visit, negotiations had taken place between the committee and Joseph Sidebotham as can be seen from a letter dated 29th March 1883 to the committee from Joseph Sidebotham.

'My Dear Dr Ransome

With reference to our conversation today about 'The Beeches'. If the committee should decide to purchase the place I will, in addition to the deduction of £1,000 from the price, give a donation of £100 in the name of my dear wife, if the committee should adopt your suggestion to call it St. Anne's Home or St. Anne's Convalescent Home or any other name in which her name should appear. I am writing to Messrs Bridgefords to tell them to withdraw the property as any day they might have arranged to sell it. The arrangements for the sale will go through their office as it is in their hands.

Believe me - yours ever truly
Joseph Sidebotham.'

It would appear that somehow the necessary capital was raised and, after an arranged meeting with Joseph Sidebotham, it was unanimously resolved that the committee should accept his offer of 'The Beeches'. On 23rd April 1884, the necessary arrangements were made for the conversion of 'The Beeches' into a hospital.

The charges at the new hospital for in-patients was 10/- per week but, for poor patients, the Secretary was to obtain what payment he could.

These gates stand today at the entrance to St Anne's Home, Woodville Road, Bowdon

The following advertisements were placed for staff:

The Manchester Hospital for Consumption and Diseases of the Throat and Chest, Bowdon, Cheshire.

Wanted an Honorary Physician. Each candidate must be registered and a Graduate in medicine of a British University or a member of The Royal College of Physicians. Applications with copies of testimonials to be sent in on or before 10 October approx.

Charles Behrens, Hon. Secretary.

*The Manchester Hospital for Consumption and
Diseases of the Throat and Chest at St Anne's Home - 1890*

**The Manchester Hospital for Consumption and Diseases of the
Throat and Chest, Bowdon, Cheshire.**

A Lady who has received thorough hospital training, is required as
Matron to superintend the nursing and management of the household.
Salary to commence at £40 per annum with board and lodgings. Apply
(with testimonials) stating age and previous experience to be sent to:

The Secretary, Consumption Hospital, St John Street, Manchester not
later than 21st inst. endorsed, application for matron.

**The Manchester Hospital for Consumption and Diseases of the
Throat and Chest, Bowdon, Cheshire.**

Wanted a qualified and registered Medical Officer for the above
institution. Salary £40 per annum with board and apartments, washing.
Applications with copies of testimonials to be sent on or before 31 July
instant.

Charles Behrens Hon. Secretary.

It is generally accepted that the Edinburgh Voluntary Tuberculosis Dispensary, which opened in 1887, was the original from which all such clinics and centres have evolved, and that the first dispensary in England was opened at Paddington in 1909. However, the opening of the Manchester Hospital for Consumption and Diseases of the Throat and Chest at St John Street, Manchester, in 1875 demonstrated that Manchester preceded Edinburgh by 12 years and Paddington by 34 years.

Two other 'pioneering' actions are also worthy of record. The Manchester Medical Officer of Health, Dr J Niven, instituted a partial system of voluntary notification of tuberculosis in 1899. The State made notification compulsory 13 years later. Manchester had a local act in 1921 giving powers of compulsory removal to hospital on public health grounds of certain types of tuberculosis patients: 15 years later, the State incorporated a similar clause in the Public Health Act of 1936.

In 1885, when 15 beds were equipped at Bowdon, the city centre hospital was replaced with a clinic on Hardman Street, which served as the out-patients department. The following letter received from John Robinson shows the respect commanded by the clinics in Hardman Street and St John Street:

'Gentlemen

I beg to return my sincere thanks for the benefit I have derived as an out and indoor patient at your valuable hospital. I particularly thank Dr Ransome for his attention and advice to me since October last. I wish also to testify to the kind treatment I have met with from Mr and Mrs McKee during the time I have been an in-patient, indeed, words would fail me to adequately express the gratitude I feel to them.

I remain   Your obedient servant John Robinson

Out-Patients Department at Hardman Street Dispensary, Deansgate, Manchester

The accommodation at Bowdon was expanded to 50 beds by the end of the century, at the expense of WJ Crossley, Chairman of the hospital and one of the Crossley Brothers - a very successful engineering firm founded in 1867. Crossley became a noted local philanthropist and, in 1906, was elected as MP for Altrincham, the constituency which included the Bowdon hospital. His wife shared his interest in tuberculosis patients, and her name was given to the Home of Peace, a large house which they provided in an industrial district of Manchester, as a refuge for advanced cases of phthisis (tuberculosis).

By 1902, partly as a result of the notification scheme, the Manchester Hospital for Consumption and Diseases of the Throat and Chest was dealing with over 11,000 cases a year - the vast majority of them seen as out-patients at the clinic in town. About 400 patients a year passed through Bowdon which, by this time, was equipped with verandas and rest-halls so that a systematic outdoor treatment could be used. The diet of patients had also been improved. Patients were visited when they went home and the poorer ones were sometimes given a daily supply of milk, eggs and rice. Tuberculosis, it was recognised, preyed on the undernourished; it was for this disease that doctors and philanthropists first attempted to ensure that patients were well nourished. The Manchester Hospital for Consumption and Diseases of the Throat and Chest, with 11,000 outpatients, had £120 per year for after-care.

It was in this environment that Withington Urban District Council commissioned the builders, Messrs TW Meadows of Stockport, to build a 100-bedded hospital on land adjoining Clay Lane and Floats Road in Baguley at a cost of approximately £60,000.

The hospital, known as Baguley Sanatorium, was built for the treatment of infectious diseases and was publicly opened on 4th October 1902 by the Rt Hon Frederick Arthur, 16th Earl of Derby, KG Lord Lieutenant of the County of Lancaster.

Waiting Hall in the Out-Patients Department at Hardman Street Dispensary

In a speech at the opening ceremonies, the Chairman, Mr Harwood, explained that the district of Withington was no longer able to send its fever patients to Monsall Hospital. Manchester Corporation now required the whole of the accommodation for their own patients, compelling Withington to make provision for itself. The institution, one of the finest of its kind in the country, was intended for the districts of Withington, Bucklow, Levenshulme and Moss

Side. The Withington District Council, however, was the controlling authority. It had always been the policy of the Council to encourage the removal to hospital of patients suffering from infectious diseases in the interest of public health, and they had paid the cost of the maintenance of patients in the hospital, irrespective of their status.

Plaque marking the Opening of Baguley Sanatorium in 1902

Mr BM Brown, in moving a vote of thanks to Lord Derby, said that, even if through the improved methods of dealing with infectious diseases, the hospital should prove too large as some people had anticipated it would do, it would still serve for a segregation sanatorium for phthisis (tuberculosis). The hospital had cost appreciably less per head than similar institutions in other parts of the country. Mr J Swarbrick, who seconded the motion, stated that the District Council had done their duty in the matter and challenged any criticism on the ground of expense.

The Lord Mayor of Manchester, in supporting the resolution, said it was seldom that the representatives of municipalities got a word of praise for the general trend of their work. He was sure the members of the Withington Council would in the long run be vindicated for their foresight.

The resolution was carried amid applause and, after Lord Derby had replied, the visitors made a thorough inspection of the sanatorium. When, in 1904, Withington was incorporated with Manchester, their recently erected sanatorium for cases of fever became one of the city hospitals.

The buildings provided 100 beds. They consisted of two two-storey pavilions, each containing 12 beds, and two single-storey pavilions each containing a 10-bedded ward. In addition, there was an 8-bedded isolation block as well as four isolation rooms attached to the two-storey pavilions. There was also an administrative block on the upper portion of the site, a farmhouse (damp and unfit for habitation), an engine house and boiler, an electrical installation consisting of a dynamo and accumulators for lighting the institution, a central heating system, disinfector, incinerator, workshops, a laundry and a mortuary. There were two approaches to the site - one off Floats Road leading to the administrative building and one in Dark Lane leading to the engine room.

16th Earl of Derby

Originally the buildings occupied an area of about 12 acres situated on a gentle slope which was open to the north and west but was partially sheltered to the south and east. The whole site extended westward from this portion along Floats Road; the sloping portion adjoining was about 8 acres in extent. Beyond these two portions lay a stretch of flat meadowland about 14 acres in extent. To the east lay a small paddock of about an acre, separated from the main site which had an area of 34 acres. The subsoil in the upper portion consisted of shale lying on clay. The meadowland was clay of great depth. To the east, the site was bordered by a stream which ran into the Fairy Well Brook, and received the effluent from the sewage works. This brook in its turn ran into a sewer which discharged into the River Mersey.

Sewage from the institution was treated via a septic tank and two successive series of four contact beds, worked automatically by a somewhat complicated system of levers. By 1906, the machinery had got out of gear, and the engineers did not or could not rectify the defects. In 1908, Dr Gilbert Fowler, on behalf of the Rivers Committee, proposed a number of improvements which were carried out, although the contact beds were never made to work successfully.

During this period, hospital provision for Manchester patients was considerably extended when WJ Crossley spent £70,000 to build a sanatorium at Delamere near Chester. It stood on a hill in countryside open to breezes from the Irish Sea. The Manchester Sanatorium had 90 beds in large, airy wards, with windows facing south which opened to allow beds to be placed on verandas. The patients spent much of their time resting on these verandas or in special shelters. The poorer patients were encouraged, where possible, to do light work around the hospital. This eased the transition from hospital to their normal working lives and was meant to ensure that they did not degenerate into chronic invalids or 'loafers'. The poorer patients were confined to the grounds which were surrounded by an unclimbable fence; the paying patients were allowed to take exercise outside. Patients could be visited once a month.

At any one time, 36 of the 90 beds were reserved for patients paying two to three guineas a week. The remaining 54 beds were occupied by 'free' patients and paid for by Manchester Corporation. The Manchester Hospital for Consumption and

Plaque as it was circa 1925 at Baguley Lodge. This plaque can be seen today on the wall near the Maternity Unit entrance. Initials in the centre denote Withington Urban District Council.

Nursing Staff at Baguley - 1921

Diseases of the Throat and Chest liked to send its curable cases to Delamere, using Bowdon for more advanced cases. In contrast, patients referred to Delamere by the Corporation were often more severe. Each patient cost about £1.13s per week (around 1906), of which almost 11s. was spent on food. (At this period, many working men earned about £1 per week, on which they were expected to feed, clothe and house a wife and several children.)

The hospital at Bowdon and the sanatorium at Delamere took a few hundred poor patients per year. The total number of beds available in voluntary and local authority hospitals was only 111, compared to 545 in Union hospitals, so that the majority of institutional care was still given under the Poor Law.

The Manchester Medical Officer for Health, Dr Niven, regretted the emphasis on treatment; in his opinion, preventive work was ultimately more useful. He was able, however, to build on the existing arrangements with the voluntary Manchester Hospital for Consumption and Diseases of the Throat and Chest by

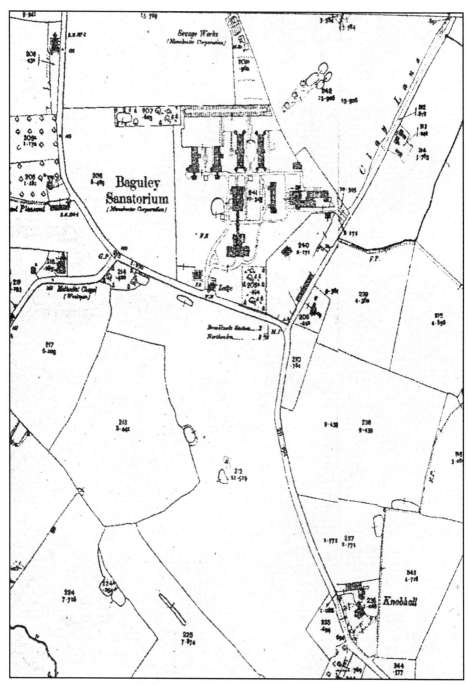

Ordnance Survey Map of Baguley 1910

appointing one of its physicians, Dr Sutherland, to be responsible for the treatment side of the city scheme. The clinic on Hardman Street was adopted as the city's tuberculosis dispensary, and Dr Sutherland's considerable clinical reputation facilitated arrangements with local medical practitioners. In 1914, Sutherland also took over responsibility for the public health work, so that he was then responsible for a service which integrated education and preventive measures, outpatient treatment and tuberculosis hospitals other than those under the Poor Law. At about the same time, the Corporation finally agreed to give support to affected families and assigned £2,000 annually. This was additional to the meagre £500 per year which had been obtained from National Insurance funds for assisting patients discharged from sanatoria.

The capital generated by National Insurance enabled Manchester Corporation to develop two additional hospital facilities - one at Baguley and the other at Abergele in North Wales. The nucleus of the Baguley scheme was conversion of the 1902 fever hospital into a sanatorium with 150 beds for the treatment of tuberculosis which opened on 8th November 1912. (In 1910, the Corporation had considered adapting it as a sanatorium but nothing was done until after the 1911 Act.) The nucleus at Abergele was a sanatorium for about fifty patients, which had been developed by the Chorlton Board of Guardians. In 1914, it was taken over by Manchester Corporation because it was government policy that the care of tuberculous patients should rest with public health authorities rather than the Poor Law, except in the case of the uninsured.

The change of use of Baguley Sanatorium meant that 100 beds for infectious diseases had to be built elsewhere. An addition was made to Monsall Hospital on the northern edge of the city - an example of rationalisation which had the usual socio-geographical consequence: a large area - in this case, south Manchester - was left without isolation facilities. Nor was the adaptation of Baguley particularly successful. There were persistent problems with sewers, building work caused prolonged disruption, and nurses were hard to find - both during the war and afterwards. By the 1920s, there were over 300 beds there. A scheme to build a working colony failed because of an argument about the site.

The patients at Baguley were mostly insured working people, and many of them did not take kindly to the hospital regime. They were not paupers, nor infected children, nor recipients of charity - as most hospital patients had been during the nineteenth century; they had paid for the services they received.

The original Baguley Sanatorium had operated as a hospital for infectious diseases from 1902 until 25th October 1912, during which time it was presided over by the Matron Superintendent assisted in turn by Dr White and Dr Tuxford. The first Medical Superintendent of the hospital was Dr Rhodes who left in 1909 and was succeeded by Dr Lister. In 1904, the Urban District Council of Withington was incorporated within the City of Manchester and control passed to the central body. Services, however, carried on as usual and during the period 1904-12 it is recorded that 4,415 cases received treatment. For the year ending December 1911, 727 patients were under treatment, 97 of whom remained in hospital on 1st January 1912. During that year, 630 patients were admitted.

The early years as a sanatorium were difficult: the only provision was the actual hospital wards. There were no outdoor shelters, proper dining rooms, or recreation rooms. Recreation was therefore restricted to such games as cards, dominoes, draughts and chess. Both acutely ill and convalescent patients were, of necessity, confined to their wards during wet or inclement weather, and, in spite of every effort to classify the patients, they frequently intermingled.

Because of the increased demand for institutional treatment throughout the country, Baguley Sanatorium had difficulty attracting experienced staff. Even

Date over the Administration Offices marking the start of building Baguley Sanatorium

34

recruiting a cook for the institution proved problematic! Another source of complaint amongst the patients in the earlier days was the absence of chaplains and religious services.

Four open-air shelters were subsequently provided, each capable of holding 18 to 20 patients. A large recreation room was temporarily provided in one of the hospital store rooms, equipped with piano, billiard table, bagatelle board and numerous games. There was a small library from which books could be borrowed twice weekly. Here the chaplains held services on Sunday afternoons. In addition to holding a service, each chaplain visited the wards once a week and at any other time if his services were desired.

In his first Annual Report, Dr James Niven MP MB LL AD stated:

"The year 1912 is is notable in the annals of the hospital because in this year it ceased to be used for infectious disease, and was converted into a Sanatorium for the treatment of tuberculosis. This report, therefore is divided into two sections: -

(i)   *The period from 1 January to 16 October, during which the hospital was used for Infectious Diseases.*
(ii)   *The period from 8 November to 31 December when Pulmonary Tuberculosis was being treated.*

The three weeks intervening between these two period were occupied by the disinfection and cleaning down of the wards and hospital generally, in preparation for the admission of tuberculosis patients.

During the year ending December 1913, 521 patients were admitted. With the 66 who remained in the hospital from 1912, a total of 587 were under treatment during the year. Of these, 391 were discharged and 57 died, leaving 131 in hospital at the end of 1913.

The State really began to take a hand in the tuberculosis problem in 1913 under the 1912 Regulations which made notification compulsory and empowered local authorities to take such steps as they considered necessary for the detection of tuberculosis and for preventing the spread of infection.

In implementing these requirements, Manchester was fortunate in having at its immediate disposal the already established out-patients department of the Manchester Hospital for Consumption and Diseases of the Throat and Chest in Hardman Street, Deansgate. Accordingly, a scheme was adopted which utilised the existing dispensary and consulting medical officers of the Consumption Hospital, with new offices built by the Corporation on adjoining land for the full time tuberculosis officers and the Corporation's administrative staff. Baguley Sanatorium was extended to accommodate 302 patients. Two new blocks for 100 male and 52 female patients were erected according to plans imposed by the Ministry of Health. The new pavilions had one and two-bedded rooms, a sub-division that permitted classification into early and more advanced cases and the reception of observation cases.

Extensive charges were made to meet the requirements of the enlarged institution. These included four new day shelters, recreation rooms and a dining hall, improvements in laundry, heating and lighting facilities and additional accommodation for medical assistants, nurses and maids. A house for the Medical Superintendent had to be built, roads had to be constructed and the grounds laid out.

Ward B4

36

The Medical Superintendent's house

In 1919, fresh problems were presented by the demand for a 56-hour week for nurses and maids. Dr RC Hutchinson presented a supplementary scheme which involved the temporary use of the isolation block as quarters for nurses and the erection of a day room. The addition of a sleeping shelter between Wards 2 and 3 increased the number of beds to 319.

Disinclination to remain in hospital for a sufficient length of time appeared to be one of the weakest points of treatment in industrial sanatoria. Many patients thought that a week or two would be sufficient to cure the disease and were keen to go home to continue as the main wage earner.

In 1913, Miss Duffill accepted the appointment of Matron, a position which she held for 25 years until her retirement in January 1938. Miss Duffill was a lady of singular charm and was liked by both patients and staff, and the familiar figure riding a tricycle about the grounds was often to be seen. In 1915 there was another change of staff, with Dr Smith succeeding Dr Lister as Medical Superintendent, a position he occupied until October, 1918. From October 1918 until the beginning of 1919, Dr Bunting occupied the position of acting Medical Superintendent, relinquishing the post on the appointment of Dr Hutchinson who carried on through the difficult post-war years until 1922 when he was succeeded by Dr Trayer.

During the First World War, the growth of the sanatorium continued despite the country's preoccupation with the conflict. In 1916, the accommodation was increased from 150 to 316 beds by the erection of Blocks 6 and 7. These buildings were of modern design and built specially to allow for the latest treatment of pulmonary tuberculosis.

Hospital Life in a Sanatorium

It may be of interest here to survey briefly the life of a patient from the time of his admission.

Shortly after arrival, the patient was seen by the Medical Superintendent or the Resident Medical Officer and allocated to one of the receiving wards. A thorough examination was made on the day following admission, after which the patient was given special instruction on precautions to be adopted and presented with a copy of the Rules and Regulations. Patients were then seen periodically by the Senior Tuberculosis Officer. For the first three days, the patient was detained in bed and a careful record made of pulse and temperature. If these were found to be normal, the patient was allowed up for a few hours. This period was steadily increased, so long as there were no adverse symptoms, until the patient was up all day. At this point, the patient entered one or other of the grades of work, which were as follows:

Class I   Walking exercise only - up to six miles daily, as directed.

Class II   Sweeping, cleaning brasses, weeding, hoeing, painting, carrying baskets of earth or cinders of about 16 lbs in weight.

Class III   Sweeping, cutting edges of lawns, digging light ground, cleaning knives and shelters. Walking two afternoons weekly.

Class IV   Small mower, rolling, wheeling barrows of grass, cinders and earth, digging, scrubbing forms and tables. Walking two afternoons weekly.

Class V   Large mower, digging heavy and unbroken land, joinering, trenching or any heavy work.

In all these grades, the routine was as follows:

7.00 am   Temperature and pulse was taken.
Half a pint of warm milk was given after which patients got up, washed and dressed, made their bed and generally helped to tidy the ward.

8.30   Breakfast was served in the dining hall.

9.00 to 9.30   Patients could spend the time as they wished, so long as they were ready for the doctor's visit at 9.30.

10.00 to 11.30   Working, exercising or resting, as ordered by the doctor.

11.30 to 12.25   Resting.

12.30	The patients prepared for dinner.
1.15 to 2.00	Patients could again amuse themselves.
2.00 to 3.30	Worked as from 10.00 to 11.30.
3.30 to 4.00	Rested on couches outdoors.
4.00	Tea.
5.00 to 7.00	Recreation was taken and temperatures were taken at 6.00 pm.
7.00	Supper was served after which patients prepared for bed.
8.30	All patients were in bed and lights are lowered.

If during the three probationary days there had been any rise of temperature, patients were kept in bed until this had absolutely settled, when they were then allowed to proceed as above.

Unfortunately, with some of the more advanced cases, the temperature never became normal. Such patients were kept continually in bed, with the exception of short journeys in a wheelchair, when their condition allowed this. So far as possible, all bed-ridden patients were moved into the open-air shelters during the daytime. The distance of the men's shelters from their wards rendered this a matter of some difficulty and only a few could be dealt with.

The daily life in the sanatorium during this period can be seen from the following letter received from Ellen Dewarrat (née Doyle):

Dear Sir

Baguley Sanatorium and Wythenshawe Hospital were on Two Different sites.

The 'Sanny', as it was called, was on the left hand side of Floats Road with a six foot wall all around it, with big iron gates. There were 4 wards, 2, 3, 4 and 5, two for males and two for females, also two called Block 6 and Block 7. The last two were known as the Veranda. They were constructed in the shape of a semi-circle with cubicles upstairs and down. The ground floors were made up of double and single cubicles , the door on one side was a single door but the doors opening out on to the lawn were made in four pieces so they were stable doors so that they could be opened to put the beds out.

The cubicle had a radiator at the foot of the bed. There were about four wool blankets and a counterpain, a hot water bottle refilled morning, noon and night.

These being the aluminium square bottled with a cover on so that one would not get burnt.

The single cubicle was given to a patient who needed treatment, namely, A.P.T., so that it was easy to bring the equipment to the patient. Patients were only put outside their cubicle at their own request and in the sunshine. I could go on forever because I have first hand information having been an inmate from 2nd February 1939 to November 1940 and then a recheck in 1941. I was the test patient for the new young doctor called Dr Hines and the first person to have two treatments at the same time, artificial pneumathorax also Gold injections .

For major surgery patients were taken to Withington for Thorocoplastic then brought back to recuperate, but such people were always on the wards, never ever on the Block. I was in when the war was declared and the hospital was taken over and we were sent to NAPTOP Sanatorium.

I was cured completely or I would not be here to tell the tale. I could give you all the details of the care and full attention I received during my stay at the "Wonderful Baguley Sanatorium".

During these long years the treatment did not change appreciably. The conservative 'fresh air' approach was considered the best method in overcoming tuberculosis, although there was some improvement in surgical treatment.

Baguley Sanatorium 1922-1940
and the contribution of Dr HG Trayer

By the end of 1922, rearrangement of the accommodation had increased the total number of beds to 333. A report by Dr HG Trayer, dated 31st December 1922, documents the increase in the number of patients admitted - 817, as compared with 741 in the previous year, with the daily average being 313.

On 31st December 1922, there were 66 patients who had been in the institution for a longer period than one year. Nine had been resident for over 5 years.

Statistics:

Patients in hospital, 1st January 1922	291
Patients admitted during the year	817*
Total patients treated	1,108
Number of patients discharged	617
Number of deaths	193
Patients remaining in hospital on 31st December 1922	291

* Includes re-admissions.

The death rate was 17.42% of the total patients treated.

In his report, Dr Trayer went on to say:

"I feel that if it were possible to separate more widely the advanced bedridden cases from the middle and early ones, the

Dr Trayer with Matron

advanced bedridden cases last days might be less bound by the restrictions that are of so much importance in the treatment and control of the latter.

The new "Day Room" for men was opened early in the year, and has proved of great value in the comfort of those patients able to enjoy its amenities. There appears to be an increase in the number of youths admitted, and if this persists it will be necessary to provide separate indoor recreational facilities for them.

Mr Chawner, Joiner, showing the Mayor some joinery produced by patients in the workshop

The new "Day Room" for females is much appreciated, though the heating by anthracite stoves is not entirely satisfactory.

The new Work Room is not yet fully equipped, but the Institutional Workshop will make the necessary articles by next winter. At present the old Day Room is used for classes and as a workroom.

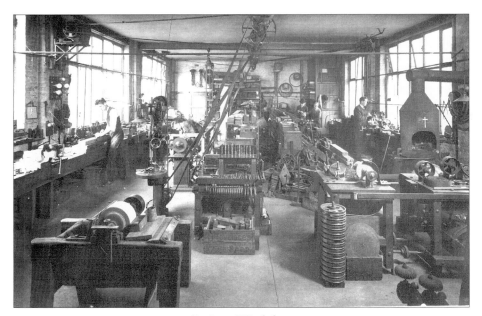

Patients' Workshop

Occupational Treatment

The Workshops still maintain their position as the most important unit in occupational treatment. I am of the opinion that it is essential that there should be a skilled joiner on the staff, who could act usually in an advisory and, if necessary, in an instructional capacity to the Carpentry section.

Handicrafts have consisted of rug making, hand weaving in wool and silk, machine knitting and macrame work. I take this opportunity of expressing my thanks to Matron, Sisters Lock and Higley, and the Head Seamstress for having rendered much valuable help. It is difficult to stimulate interest in the average patient, and even when enthusiasm is aroused, to maintain it until a practical working knowledge is attained, and the appointment of a Vocational Sister should be seriously considered, whose duty it would be to teach, collectively and individually, useful handicrafts.

Lectures have been given regularly to all male patients on the elementary hygiene of tuberculous.

Recreation Hall - now demolished - which doubled as the Chapel
Note the Cross on the second story end wall.)

Entertainments

On behalf of the patients and staff I wish to express our grateful thanks to Messrs. Gaumont Limited for the weekly supply of films during the winter months.

The weekly concerts have been much appreciated, and our thanks are due to many professionals and amateurs who have so readily given their services.

The fortnightly whist drives have been very popular.

In conclusion, I wish to express my thanks to all members of the staff for the loyal and willing manner in which their duties have been carried out."

In 1931, the pressure on Baguley beds had to be eased by transferring some patients to Withington Hospital. Three years later, land was allocated for extensions at Baguley Sanatorium and, in 1935, a scheme first raised in 1926 was approved by Manchester Corporation. This increased the capacity by 84 beds for females and a home for 91 nurses on the south side of Floats Road.

Staffing problems occurred in 1936 and 1937 due in part to the reduction of nurses' working hours from 48 to 40 a week. At the time, questions were raised as to how the nurses would spend all their additional spare time! Domestic staff did not have any extra time off because they had a weekend off every other week.

One man more than any other personified the spirit of Baguley Sanatorium. This man was Dr Trayer who was Medical Superintendent of Baguley from 1922 to his retirement in 1954.

Hugh George Trayer was born in Dublin in 1889 and educated at Oswestry and Trinity College, Dublin, where he took his BA in 1911 and his MB BCh the following year.

Dr Hugh G Trayer

His first involvement with tuberculosis was in 1913 when, after taking his Diploma in Public Health at the University of Manchester, he received his certificate of postgraduate training in tuberculosis.

From September 1912 to March 1913, he was Junior House Surgeon at Stockport Infirmary, moving from there to spend six months at Monsall Fever Hospital. The first six months of 1914 he spent at sea, as Ship's Surgeon with the Blue Funnel Line. After a further month as House Surgeon at Salford Royal Infirmary, he was posted to the Sheffield Royal Army Medical Corps depot. It was during this period that he was awarded the Serbian Order of the White Eagle with Swords and he was mentioned in dispatches in 1918. After the evacuation, he was drafted to France and Belgium. In 1919, he left the Army with the rank of Major.

In September 1919, he began his long association with Baguley Sanatorium as Senior Medical Officer. He left briefly to become Medical Superintendent of Romsley Hill Sanatorium, Halesowen, and, in February 1922, returned to

Mr Graham Bryce   Dr Trayer   Mr Graham Bryce

Baguley as Medical Superintendent. During the 32 years that he was associated with Baguley, he made particular contributions to raising the standards of nursing in tuberculosis.

When Dr Trayer retired in 1954, Dr JR Sinton gave the following appreciation:

"For many years now, newcomers to Baguley, whether patients or staff, have quickly come to realise that the presiding genius of the place is a distinguished, white-coated figure, erect in carriage, rolled umbrella on arm, collar turned up, and small brown box in his hand, walking serenely from ward to ward.

Dr Trayer's retirement this summer ends an association of thirty-five years, and though we grieve to see him leave us, we can but wish him every possible happiness and the enjoyment of long years which his work here has so richly earned him.

He came here as Resident Medical Officer, after distinguished service from 1914-19 with the R.A.M.C., in the Dardenelles, Egypt and France, as well as sundry adventures as shops' surgeon, sailing to Far Eastern waters. He left for a year to be superintendent of a smaller hospital near Birmingham, and returned to be Medical Superintendent of Baguley Sanatorium in October 1922. He has remained to change the former fever hospital of the urban district of Withington in to the maze of buildings which forms Baguley Hospital, Wythenshawe

Baguley Ward built circa 1900

Hospital (formerly Baguley Emergency Hospital) and the Nurses' Home, and serves a region of 4,000,000 people.

Designs and plans have been his concern over the years; to modify the existing structures so that they could meet the changing methods of treatment, but to preserve his fundamental concepts of rest, moving air, a nourishing diet, and a gradual restoration to a normal or modified healthy life. The joinery shop was, in its day, a pioneer effort, and the Sanatorium bowling team could take on all comers. With the passing years, occupational therapy has had to come to the patient in his bed, bowling is a skill practiced on other greens, and surgery with its bustle and drama has replaced some of the methods once used in the treatment of tuberculosis.

Doctor Trayer has been a pioneer, too, in his weekly broadcast talks to give patients an idea of the problems they must face and the ways by which these may be overcome, and he was one of the first to recognise that tuberculous patients need specialised nursing. He played a large part in obtaining recognition for the training nurses undergo in sanatoria, and has always worked to raise the standard of that training. In a service which has been subject to parsimonious economy of management, he has remained the idealist striving after the best, yet realistically seizing the smallest opportunity to achieve some permanent gain.

Patients taking in fresh air on the veranda

Yet it is not only for these things that he will be remembered here. His knowledge and concern for the individual patients under his care (and there have been nearly 18,000 during these years) have been the touchstone of his success. Their needs, anxieties, perversities, and successes, have been his first concern. For him the organisation is only the means whereby men and women can be restored in health to their homes and families, and for this alone he has given so freely of his talents and strength. He has been helped unfailingly by Mrs Trayer who has supported him ably in all his work and has often spent long days and nights in preparation of some special festive occasion."

Thirty-two years is a considerable slice of a man's life and, when reflecting on his period at Baguley, Dr Trayer made the following observations:

"Looking back one realises how much was done with so little. In the old days the tempo of life in a sanatorium was slow and peaceful; there was a sense of

Open-air wards for tuberculosis patients

restfulness and ordered routine. Here at Baguley no scientifically prepared product was disregarded without trial, nor was any procedure left untried.

"Many of them would not be tried to-day without radiological control, and yet in the past that control was not always available. Twenty-five years ago the X-ray report mentioned that 812 patients were screened, and 35 were photographed. Last year there were nearly 5,000 screenings and 7,000 X-ray pictures.

".....but happiness was conspicuous by its presence, and self pity and fear conspicuous by their absence. No one would wish for the old days to return, but one would wish for the restoration of that spirit of service which pervaded this community in the days of long ago, but which to-day exists only among the few."

"And the future: 'Much can be done by teaching positive health ... that prevention is better than cure, and that tuberculosis is not a dishonourable disability, but a disability that may well have been due to the stress and strain in the battle of everyday life.

"There seems little doubt that we can expect further developments in the field of research, the production of better and safer drugs applicable to all types of disease. As the health of the nation rises, and when healthy living becomes more important than the treatment of disease, then and then only will this social evil, tuberculosis, be on its way out.""

The July 1954 edition of *San Toy,* the house magazine of Baguley Sanatorium, contained the following message from the Lord Mayor of Manchester, Alderman Richard S Harper JP:

"It is with great pleasure, and a sense of some regret, that I write this introduction to the Farewell Edition of San Toy. Pleasure because of my long personal association with Doctor Trayer, and regret that Baguley Sanatorium is losing one who has been associated for so long with so much of its progress. Doctor Trayer has been Physician Superintendent of Baguley Sanatorium for thirty-two years, during which time he has worked successfully to achieve two main objects - a recognition of the needs of the tuberculosis service, and the building up of a community spirit within the Sanatorium, a spirit aimed largely at removing the now happily dying social stigma which was once associated with the disease. He has brought the name of Baguley Sanatorium, Manchester, to a point where is it respected and admired in medical and social circles, and he has lost no opportunity, both at local and national level, to further the cause of tuberculosis service. I am sure that readers of San Toy will join me in thanking Doctor Trayer for his works in connection with the fight against tuberculosis in Manchester, wishing him and Mrs Trayer a successful and happy retirement.

The July 1954 edition of the *San Toy* magazine included Dr Trayer's reply in the form of a goodbye message:

'The Chief' says Goodbye

As a Forward to the first number of San Toy in August 1935, I expressed the hope that this magazine, for the patients by the patients, would further extend the spirit of helpfulness, kindliness and good humour which pervaded this place. I think that even though San Toy has had its ups and downs it has helped to maintain this spirit. On reflection it is obvious that life is a long series of goodbyes - not necessarily to people, but to those hopes and aspirations which, perchance, may well have been only dreams, but which remorseless time decrees can never be fulfiled. It has been written that Christianity cannot take the place of thinking, but it must be founded on it. I have striven over the years that are past to adopt, in the very broadest sense, this principle, realising that in seeking the greatest happiness for the greatest number, it was necessary to control this community in the guise of a benevolent dictator. Whether this system has succeeded must be judged by those who have been subjected to it. Bacon wrote: "The greatest trust between man and man is the trust of giving counsel." It is a great consolation to me that so many have trusted me in this sense and taken that counsel. There will be one indelible memory that I take with me - the courage of the ordinary man and woman when fighting this disabling disease, and even though modern treatment can do so much more than long ago, it will still be necessary to face the danger without fear. This place has never striven for anything other than the good of the community, and perhaps that verse of Rudyard Kipling epitomises what was in my mind and heart many years ago:

> *In all our time of distress*
> *and in our triumph too*
> *The game is more than the player of the game,*
> *And the ship is more than the crew.*

To all those who are and who have been members of this community, I say "Farewell, may God be with you.""

An element of Dr Trayer's character is described in a letter from Maureen Fitzgibbon of Altrincham, later Lady Mayoress of Manchester, who had a four-week spell in hospital in 1947:

"As far as I recall, the Medical Superintendent, Dr Trayer, was responsible for most of the medical treatment and the patients were very much in awe of him. I think that they were taken over to a clinic building to see him. He certainly held weekly screening clinics to which all the patients with artificial pneumothoracs were taken. These were quite social occasions where patients, male and female, from all the wards fraternised. This was, of course, quite illegal. Dr Trayer sat behind the screen, flanked by junior medical staff, and saw every patient and made decisions about treatment.

Dr Trayer could be quite stern with patients who were failing to make progress or who were mis-behaving and tales about his comments were passed around. One of his pet treatments for patients who he thought had developed tuberculous laryngitis (and there seemed to be quite a few) was to put them on 'silence' or 'whispers'. At the screening sessions it was reputed that he would ask the silent ones how they were and if they replied were soundly told off for speaking! Being up-graded from silence to whispers was a great sign of improvement.

Hugh George Trayer died on 4th January 1975 at the age of 85. His obituary in the *British Medical Journal* said:

"Dr Trayer will be remembered with feelings of admiration and affection by the many middle aged and elderly doctors and patients who benefited by his life".

Hospital Standing Orders and Rules and Regulations

Both patients and staff were subject to strict discipline and regulations as can be seen from the following extracts from the hospital's Standing Orders. These extracts also give some idea of what it must have been like in the hospital through the 1930s:

31st May 1929

There appears to be some misconception of the carrying out of "Absolute Rest". The nursing of cases on absolute rest will bear no deviation from its strict routine without written instructions on the chart from the Medical Officer in charge of the Ward in each particular case, and sisters in charge of Wards will instruct individual members of their staff in the correct carrying out of this most important form of treatment.

The practice of allowing "Absolute" patients to get out, or to be lifted out of bed during bed making and other such proceedings is forbidden. It is to be noted that patients in this Sanatorium, when on absolute rest, are allowed - when able - to feed themselves, to receive visitors, to write not more than one letter per day, and to read for short periods at a time. Patients on absolute rest are to be dissuaded from trying to obtain articles for themselves from their lockers, and female patients may not sew or knit continuously.

Attention is again directed towards the Notes on Ward Administration for the Guidance of the Nursing Staff, particularly that part referring to rest.

It is also to be noted that there is not sufficient supervision of the Rest Hours for up patients - these must be strictly and correctly adhered to. Patients who do not carry out this important feature of their treatment must be reported to the Medical Officer in charge of the Ward.

By Order Medical Superintendent.

Wards 6A and 6B

The weekly cleaning of wards will take place on Saturday mornings or Friday afternoons, except in such instances as are otherwise detailed.

ALL PATIENTS who do their wards on Friday afternoons will attend handicrafts on Saturday mornings. When leave is granted for a Saturday, the cleaning will be done on Friday morning or afternoon. Those patients on Handicrafts will notify the Instructor on the Thursday as to which session they will be absent, and will attend a corresponding session on the Friday afternoon or morning.

Wards 4 and 5

All patients on Graduated Exercise or Handicrafts will attend for handicrafts on Saturday mornings. Those usually on one hour craft from 9.30 to 10.30, all others from 10.0 to 11.25.

General

Walks. In future the days for walks will be detailed by the Medical Officers. Patients on walks "A" to "D" will have one hour allotted, and the times for male patients will be:

If in the mornings	*10.30 to 11.30*
If in the afternoons	*2.00 to 3.00*
Patients on Walk "E"	*10.20 to 11.30*
or	*2.00 to 3.10*

It will be noted that the time for the hot fore-noon drink for "up" patients will be 10.25 to 10.35. This will allow the majority of patients on crafts to have this drink after or before their particular session.

Those patients on various graduated exercises will be allowed a few minutes break to go to their wards at 10.30 - except those on the Dining Hall. Arrangements for Saturday morning craft session will be made in due course.

In order to clear up a very obvious misconception, it is pointed out that patients on Grades I, II and III do not cease until the buzzer goes at 11.40 in the mornings and at 3.20 in the afternoons. Those on Grades IV and V cease at 11.55 and 3.50.

Patients with Yellow or Red cards on returning from a walk on ordinary days will proceed to Rest at 11.30 or 3.30 as the case may be. The privilege of being allowed out on a Saturday afternoon from 1.0 to 6.30 remains for those patients on Tables "B" and "C".

Patients with Yellow cards (Table "B") can go for a walk on Sunday mornings 10.30 to 11.30 and Sunday afternoons 2.0 to 3.0. Patients on Table "C" can go for a walk on Sunday mornings from 10.30 to 11.30 and in the afternoons from 2.0 to 3.50.

The foot notes at end of Routine on the back of Yellow and Red cards are herewith cancelled.

All patients will rest from 11.30 to 12.20 on Saturdays and Sundays. All patients on Table "B" or "C", who are at present on Special graduated exercise in the mornings only, will in future attend Grades or Handicrafts in the afternoons.

Patients attending crafts from 2.0 to 4.0 will take their mugs with them so as to proceed direct to the Dining Hall.

Patients on 6 and 8 hours who are put on Handicrafts, will report to the Instructor at 1.30 p.m. on the same day. Patients on 10 and 12 hours put on Handicrafts, will report to the Instructor at 9.30 a.m. on the next day.

Additional and supplementary Rest periods may be prescribed in individual cases even though the individual should be on Table "B" or "C". The time allotted to Rest will not be affected by Visiting Day. All patients will co-operate and assist the Staff in ensuring that this Scheme runs smoothly from the commencement.

By Order Medical Superintendent.

2nd April 1931

There appears to be some necessity to offer guidance on the question of providing the nearest relatives of patients on the List with refreshments during the period of day duty. It will be noted that for relatives staying overnight, adequate arrangements are in practice and have been found satisfactory.

It is suggested that in most cases the provision of a cup of tea and some bread and butter in the ward kitchen is adequate, but this must be confined to the nearest relative, and only in exceptional cases must this privilege be extended to two relatives, and this number must not be exceeded. If, in the Ward sister's or her deputy's opinion, something more substantial than the above is necessary (but each case must be considered strictly upon its merits), the following arrangements can be made for the nearest relative to have a meal in the Rest Room; such meal will be confined to the mid-day dinner period (12.00 noon to 2.0 p.m.), and only in exceptional cases at any other time.

A note, signed and dated by the Sister or Nurse in charge of the ward, will be sent to the Still Room and the relative will be sent to the Rest Room:

This procedure is an endeavour to avoid the necessity of having to supply food other than tea and bread and butter on the ward. It is particularly requested that the most stringent instructions be given that this privilege is not to be abused, as it is not my intention that there should be any question of right of relative to receive refreshments while visiting here, but, on the other hand, I feel that in certain cases it is a very real necessity which in the past has been somewhat haphazardly provided for but is now put upon a basis that should commend itself to all.

HG Trayer Medical Superintendent.

25th September 1931

As there appears to be some misunderstanding concerning certain matters, the following is published for the information of all patients on Wards 6A and 6B:

Patients are expected to keep their wards in the first place - TIDY. Even patients confined to bed can materially aid in this object by having the minimum number of articles behind their bed rests.

Patients receiving visitors at any time will see that they do not sit upon the bed; bedside chairs are primarily for sitting upon and the lockers furnish another convenient seat.

Patients are not allowed (according to rule 17) to introduce any food into the Sanatorium except fruit. Fruit is not to be kept in the locker, which is provided for the storing of clothes and small personal effects (exception will be made in the case of sugar).

Patients are not allowed tea after dinner.

Special boxes for the storage of cleaning material (e.g. polish etc.) will be provided shortly. Brushes, mops, buckets, etc., will not be kept in the wards under any consideration whatsoever.

The practice of bed patients having urinals constantly in the wards will cease forthwith. Those patients who have received permission from the medical officer to have urinals for the night will not keep them in their wards during the day time. The urinals will be returned to whatever sluice room the nurse in charge decides is the most convenient.

The attention of the staff is directed to the above and, in addition, to the importance of seeing that each patient has a bed ticket properly filled in, and that bed ticket holders are not used for hanging Burney Yeo Inhalers, etc., upon, but that the holder and ticket are at all times plainly visible. Le Duc's tubes are not to be kept by the patient behind his bed rest. The supply and use of Orthoform will be supervised with the utmost economy - this is an exceedingly expensive drug, yet every patient on Orthoform is to have sufficient.

The bed side chairs are primarily for the use of patients' visitors to sit upon; therefore, on visiting day, they should be clear, but at the same time, everything removed from them is not to be placed behind the bed rest.

> *Medical Superintendent.*

21st February 1933

Eggs

All hospital eggs issued to Wards in lieu of bacon will be marked with the name of the patient and the number of the ward, and taken to the Patients' Dining Hall by the Wardmaid at 7.45 a.m. This instruction applies to Dining Hall patients only.

Ward tidiness

Chairs must not be used as boot and shoe racks, nor must electric light fittings or door fittings be used for hanging coats, hats, etc., upon. Patients are not allowed to drive nails in the walls or stick pictures upon the walls. Surplus clothing, previously checked in the presence of the Sister in charge of the Ward, can be placed in suit cases, etc., and stored for patients.

Notice to Ward Sisters

Entertainments - When there are entertainments for patients (e.g. pictures) from 4.30 p.m. to 6.30 p.m. suppers will be drawn, delivered and served to Bed Patients at the usual time. Supper will be served in the Dining Hall at the conclusion of the entertainment. This is to enable the Day Staff to be ready at 7.25 to take the temperatures and pulses of all patients who have been to the entertainment.

In the event of patients on two or four hours receiving the permission of the Medical Officer in charge of the ward to attend the entertainment, they will be instructed to have their supper in the Dining Hall.

Sisters in charge of wards will make a special note on the diet sheet for the day of those patients who will be extra for supper in the Dining Hall.

Medical Superintendent

3rd August 1933

To Sisters in charge of Wards

After careful observation and due consideration, it is necessary to bring to the notice of all members of the nursing staff the laxity and the apparent lack of appreciation of the importance of giving proper information as to the condition of patients. It is noted that in some cases when enquiries are made about individual patients the nursing staff reply that there is no such patient on the ward; yet, in one particular case, the patient had been on the ward for six months. Also, such replies as 'The patient is all right' is not in accordance with

59

the past reputation for accuracy of information concerning patients that this Sanatorium has acquired. Those patients whose names are on the Seriously and Dangerously Ill lists are not really the patients concerned in this note. It is the enquiries about other patients where care should be taken, and it should be remembered that, with recent admissions, it is quite reasonable to expect the relatives to inquire the day the patient is admitted as to how the patient is. Information concerning patients not on the List should be expressed by such wording as 'He/she is quite comfortable'. On the other hand, if, for example, a patient has not been quite so well and has been returned to bed, that could be covered by the statement that the patient 'has not been quite so well today'.

Enquiries from the Lodge should be most courteously and fully replied to, as frequently the member of the staff has no idea for whom the information is required.

Notice to Patients

In order to suit the convenience of patients proceeding on pass, breakfast in future on pass days will be served in the dining hall at 8.0 a.m. The first buzzer will sound at 7.45 a.m. and the second buzzer at 8.00 a.m. This should prevent any undue strain of hurrying for the bus.

Patients are reminded that these arrangements do not mean that they are to leave their beds and wards in any other condition but that of tidiness and cleanliness.

Medical Superintendent

9th October 1936

Notice to Patients

There does not appear to have been any appreciable economy exercised in the use of water since my last instructions.

It is again pointed out that some of the principal ways in which water is wasted are as follows:

Taps not being completely turned off after use.

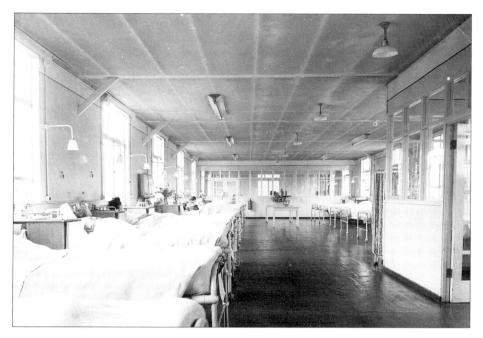

A typical ward during rest period

Allowing hot water taps to run for some considerable time before using.
(The failure of the hot water system to supply hot water will be reported at once.)
Failing to report inefficient taps.
Washing under running water.
Failing to put plug in basin or bath while washing or shaving.
Filling hot water bottles at places other than those specially
provided for the purpose.

Wards 6A and 6B. The practice of swilling out the cubicles will be substituted by the use of deck scrubbers and mops, and the minimum amount of water will be used even for this practice. The cleanliness of a floor does not depend upon the amount of water that is swilled over it.

The washing of the Dining Hall floor and the Billiards Room will be carried out with the most careful regard to these instructions.

Medical Superintendent

17th November 1937

Notice to Sister in charge of the ward and for the information of all Nursing Staff

There does not appear to be sufficient attention paid to the privilege of patients' visitors.

When a patient obtains special permission for visitors to come in on a day and time other than the normal visiting day, this permission must be notified to the Lodge by the ward.

Casual and emergency visitors will be allowed when they are in possession of the special permit initialled by a Medical Officer.

Requests for alteration of the visiting permit to any other day will in all cases be done through the Medical Superintendent's office.

As there are so many patients having the same surname, and in many cases the same initials, it is essential that the full christian names and surnames be inscribed on all ordinary visiting cards.

When visitors have lost the ordinary visiting card, under no circumstances will a new one be issued by the ward. The visitors must be informed that they must apply in writing to the Medical Superintendent for a new card.

There is no alteration as regards visiting of patients placed on the daily visiting list. The attention of all members of nursing staff is drawn to the fact that the Lodge must be made aware, in so far as it concerns the Lodge Keeper, of special and other visitors.

It is realised that there is considerable difficulty at times in controlling the two visitors per patient on visiting days but the nursing staff must not relax their vigilance in the matter under any circumstances whatsoever. It seems hardly necessary to point out how unfair it is to those patients who conform to rules, to allow other patients to break them.

Medical Superintendent

Segregation of the sexes appeared to be of major importance as illustrated by the following notice relative to the use of the Recreation Hall issued on 9th October 1936

"Female patients will approach the Hall by the path running alongside Ward 2, and on entering the Hall by the middle door will occupy the seats on the right hand side of the Hall facing the stage commencing on the front row. At the end of a performance female patients will leave the Hall by the centre door on the north side, turn to the right and return to their wards by the same way as they came.

Male patients will approach the Hall by the roadway between Wards 3 and 4, entering the Hall by the first door (nearest to the stage). They will occupy the seats on the left hand side of the Hall facing the stage as directed by the Stewards. Male patients may leave at the end of the performance either by the door they entered by or by the middle door on the same side.

The doors for the admission of patients will be closed promptly either when the performance starts or, in the case of cinema shows, at the advertised time of commencement, and will be opened for late comers at the end of the first item.

All patients are requested to avail themselves of the scrapers and mats provided on the slipways outside the doors. Smoking is prohibited.

Patients attending concerts, cinema shows, whist drives, etc., are not to throw rubbish of any description on the floor of the Hall. Patients eating wrapped sweets should have with them a receptacle to put the wrappings in. The door at the chancel end (which is reserved for staff only to enter by) will remain open during a performance, and any person wishing to leave the Hall during a performance will use this door.

If the necessity of emptying the Hall rapidly should arise, the general rule to be adopted is that all persons on the South side (i.e., left side facing the stage) will leave by the nearest door on that side and, those on the North side, by the nearest door on that side. Under such conditions all patients will immediately return to their respective wards by the ordinary route.

Medical Superintendent

The rules and regulations remained much the same over the years as can be seen from the following 1947 list:

1. *Every patient is expected to provide warm clothing, as directed on the slips accompanying the intimation of admission. All such clothing must be plainly marked. Unmarked clothes must be shown to the Sister in charge of the ward immediately after admission, when arrangements will be made to mark them.*

2. *A copy of the Daily Routine will be given to each patient on admission, and must be strictly adhered to.*

3. *Patients will at all times behave in a quiet and orderly manner. Shouting, whistling and running is forbidden.*

4. *Every patient who is sufficiently well will take a bath on admission, and at least one a week during his stay. Bath nights and hours to be fixed by the Ward Sister.*

BAGULEY SANATORIUM
GENERAL ROUTINE FOR PATIENTS IN BED
AND LESS THAN TWELVE HOURS.

a.m.
6 0   Temperatures taken. Morning tea. Wash.
8 15   Breakfast.
9 0   Patients on 10 hours rise.
9 30—10 30   Handicraft.
10 25 or 10 35   Hot drink.
10 30   Prescribed activity—handicraft or ward.
11 30—12 20   Rest.
12 20   Patients on 1 to 8 hours rise.
12 30   Dinner
1 15   Patients on 1 hour retire to bed.
1 0—1 25   Rest—6 and 8 hourly patients.
1 30—2 30   Handicraft—6 and 8 hourly patients only.
1 15—1 50   Rest
2 0—3 20   Prescribed activity—handicraft or ward.
2 30—3 0   Rest—6 and 8 hourly patients.
3 0   Patients on 2 hours retire to bed.
3 40—4 0   Rest.
4 0   Tea.
4 30   Patients on 4 hours retire to bed.
5 0   Temperatures taken for all patients now in bed.
5 30—6 15   Rest. Temperatures taken.
6 30   Supper.
7 0   Patients on 6 hours retire to bed.
*8 30   Hot drink. Patients retire to bed.
*9 0   Lights out. No talking.
* These times will be half-an-hour later during the summer months.
Patients will observe all the Rules and Regulations.
There will be no talking, reading, writing, or smoking during Rest periods, which must be rigidly adhered to.
Patients may listen to the wireless.
This routine is subject to variation for individual patients as the Medical Officer prescribes.

Corporation of Manchester

Baguley Sanatorium

Rules & Regulations

FOR

Patients

Name of Patient:

1947

5. *Every bed patient will be provided with a sputum box and those on hours with a sputum flask, and must always use same, as instructed, for the disposal of sputum. Refusal to do this will lead to discharge.*

6. *All patients medically fit, will be required to make their own beds on rising in the morning, and may be required to assist in making those of more weakly patients before going to breakfast. Lockers must be kept clean and tidy, and they may be inspected at any time by the Medical Officer, Sister or Nurse in charge of the ward.*

7. *The "buzzer" will be sounded fifteen minutes before breakfast and again at 8.30. Patients must make themselves clean and tidy before proceeding to meals. At all other meals only one "buzzer" will be sounded.*

8. *It is essential that the hands should be carefully washed before meals, as owing to the constant use of the sputum flask and pocket handkerchief the fingers are contaminated with the germs of Tuberculosis, and these, if taken into the mouth with food, may give rise to further infection.*

9. *The proper ventilation of all wards, recreation rooms, dining hall and handicraft departments is of the greatest importance. Patients are forbidden to close windows or ventilators that have been opened by members of Staff except when rain or snow is driving in.*

10. *The Medical Officer of the ward prescribes such handicrafts, ward duties, graduated exercises and rest periods as are suitable to the medical condition of each individual patient. The importance of carrying out this part of the treatment in every detail cannot be too strongly emphasized. It is only by a combination of rest and controlled effort that the highest attainable degree of health can be reached.*

11. *Smoking is very undesirable as it tends to increase cough and expectoration, and may therefore do harm. All patients are advised to give it up if possible. Under no circumstances must patients smoke in the wards, bath-room or dining hall. Cigarette ends, matches, waste paper, dregs, fruit peel, etc., must not be thrown on the ground, but placed in the receptacle provided.*

12. *No games may be indulged in except during the time that is allotted to recreation. Violent or exciting games are forbidden.*

13. *Betting or gambling is forbidden and offenders will be discharged forthwith.*

14. *Patients desirous of playing musical instruments, in order to entertain bed patients, must obtain permission from the Ward Sister, and such entertainment will only be allowed during recreation hours.*

15. *Swearing or the use of improper language is strictly forbidden. Any familiarity between male and female patients is strictly forbidden, or between patients and any member of the Staff and will lead to the discharge of the offenders.*

16. *On no account must alcohol or medicines be introduced into the Sanatorium.*

17. *Patients are amply fed and no food may be brought into the Sanatorium without permission, and this will be confined to butter, eggs, sugar, fruit and possibly jam.*

18. *Patients must enter and leave the Sanatorium by the MAIN ENTRANCE only and must be in possession of a 'Pass' or 'Grade Card' signed by a Medical officer. Patients must not walk across flower beds, lawns or shrubberies and the picking of flowers is forbidden.*

19. *Visiting days are alternative Saturdays from 1.15 to 4 p.m., and alternate Sundays from 2 to 4 p.m. The number of visitors allowed is as stated on the visiting permit. All visitors must be clear of the gates at 4 p.m. No visitors are allowed at other times unless a possession of a 'Pass' signed by the Medical Superintendent.*

20. *Any patient wishing to see the Medical Superintendent or the Medical Officer on duty, should report to the Sister or Nurse in charge of the ward, when the necessary arrangements for any interview will be made.*

21. *Patients' underclothing will be washed in the Hospital Laundry, and the details of articles must be plainly indicated on the Laundry Slips. The soiled handkerchiefs of patients who are up must be placed in the special bags provided on each ward.*

22. Responsibility will not be accepted for any money or valuables unless handed to the Sister in charge of the ward, and a receipt given for sale.

   No responsibility is accepted for patients' clothing

23. Patients will at all times observe the notices and instructions issued, from time to time, by the Medical Superintendent.

   By Order Medical Superintendent

Baguley Emergency Services

With the increasing tension in Europe during 1937-39, the possibility of a second European war could not be ignored. The Spanish Civil War had demonstrated the need to defend the civilian population against aerial attack and to provide treatment for casualties. Early in 1938, medical officers of the Ministry of Health surveyed the existing hospital accommodation in England and Wales, and recorded 3,128 hospitals and institutions containing 400,000 to 500,000 beds, of which 130,000 were in mental hospitals. Hospitals were divided into two categories: voluntary and municipal. The former class comprised general hospitals, infectious diseases hospitals, tuberculosis sanatoria and maternity and child welfare institutions financed by Ministry grants and local rates. Prior to June 1938, local authorities were required to provide accommodation for the treatment of casualties as part of their air-raid precautions. In June 1938, the Ministry of Health assumed responsibility.

It had been estimated that, in the event of war, immediate accommodation should be available for 300,000 civilian casualties, in addition to possible

Baguley Sanatorium in the 1940s with EMS huts to be seen at top right hand corner

requirements of the armed forces. This was to be done in three ways: by discharging all ambulance patients and those who could safely be sent home, thus clearing about 100,000 beds; by 'crowding' hospitals with 110,000 extra beds, and, by building new hutted hospitals to hold 90,000 beds. When the war broke out, the Emergency Medical Services (EMS) had retained 2,370 hospitals with 309,354 beds suitable for casualties. Within a week, 'crowding' had provided 187,000 extra beds.

When the expected aerial bombardment did not materialise, a number of hospitals were released for the treatment of ordinary civilian sick. By January 1940, there were 1,207 hospitals remaining in the scheme with 262,859 beds for casualties. By the end of 1942, a further reduction left 892 hospitals and institutions with 278,761 beds. The numbers then remained fairly constant, but from 1945 onwards there was a steady decline. By the end of 1947, 329 hospitals were left in service containing 18,000 beds which were, however, available for ordinary civilian use when not required for EMS patients. The Emergency Hospital Services were finally merged with the National Health Service in July 1948.

In addition to ordinary facilities for the treatment of casualties, about 120 special centres were set up - either as separate hospitals or as wings of existing hospitals. These provided treatment facilities for orthopaedic surgery (20), skin diseases

Emergency Medical Services Huts

69

(20), neurosis (14), maxillo-facial injuries (12), head injuries (11) and chest injuries (10).

The main classes of EMS patients were:

a)   Civilians, including regular police, suffering from war injuries and injuries incurred in the performance of Civil Defence duties.

b)   Service men and women, whether sick or injured, including repatriated prisoners-of-war as well as Dominion and Allied Forces and their auxiliary medical personnel.

c)   Merchant Navy officers and men.

d)   Evacuee children, refugees from Gibraltar and the Channel Islands, sick civilians moved from target areas, transferred war workers and those in agricultural or forestry camps.

e)   Persons who, in the interest of the war effort, needed to be restored to health and full working capacity as quickly as possible - notably cases of fractures and certain other types of injury occurring among manual workers in factories and full-time Civil Defence workers.

Aerial view of the EMS huts

One of the EMS hospitals was built on the Baguley site next to the older tuberculosis wards. In 1939, before the outbreak of war, Manchester Corporation began to erect a temporary hutted hospital in the grounds of Baguley Sanatorium to receive air-raid casualties from Manchester as part of the Emergency Medical Services. Several of the wooden huts were built in 1940 and, when the fall of Norway put timber in short supply, they were completed as brick structures and became known as Baguley Emergency Hospital.

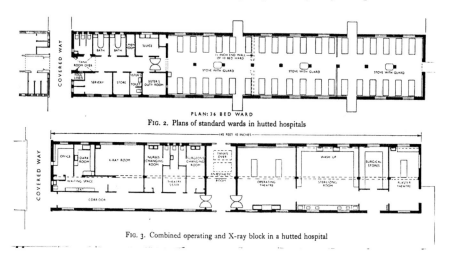

FIG. 2. Plans of standard wards in hutted hospitals

FIG. 3. Combined operating and X-ray block in a hutted hospital

Plan of X-ray block in a hutted ward

The Baguley Emergency Hospital comprised 17 pavilions with theatre and radiological units, kitchens, stores, dining and recreation rooms and office accommodation. It initially had a capacity of 680 beds, though this was reduced to 350 in view of the specialist nature of the units and the need for space for other services, such as physiotherapy and occupational therapy. Special hostels were built near the Sanatorium Nurses Home to accommodate the Baguley Emergency Hospital nursing staff.

Following the Department of Health's appointment of Sir Harold Gillies and Sir Kelsey Fry in 1938 as advisors to organise the development of maxillo-facial and plastic surgery centres, peripheral centres were established throughout the country. In Manchester, a unit was established at the EMS Hospital under the inspired leadership of Professor FC Wilkinson (an Australian by birth and the

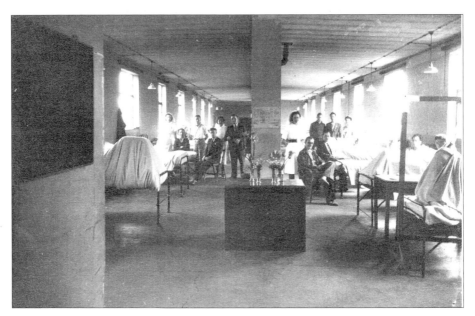

Pavilion 1947 showing the coke fire with its chimney that provided heating

Dean of the Dental School) who himself had worked with Gillies and Fry at Sidcup after the First World War.

At the outbreak of the war, all the civilian tuberculosis patients were moved out of Baguley Sanatorium to make way for the anticipated war casualties. A dental laboratory was set up on one of the ward verandas. The EMS Division of the Ministry of Health supplied surgical kits to stock the theatres and departments in the new EMS hospital that was under construction. The Plastic Surgery and Maxillo-Facial Unit was staffed in 1940 by Professor Wilkinson and Professor Matthews from the Dental School, with FH Bentley responsible for plastic surgery and Alan Weldon Moule responsible for oral surgery.

The first patients were received from Dunkirk on 3rd June 1940. They were a party of 10 patients with maxillo-facial injuries sent from the receiving hospital at Calderstone in Central Lancashire. At that time, there was one ward for officers and one ward for other ranks.

The nursing personnel consisted of four state registered nurses assisted by several Red Cross nurses and anaesthesia was supplied by doctors from surrounding hospitals.

In 1941, the unit moved into the new EMS Hospital that had been built adjacent to the sanatorium. In that year, FH Bentley was called up for army service and his place was taken by Dr John Marquis Converse from New York, transferred as part of the American Hospital in Great Britain. He was accompanied by Mr Jimmy Weeks, his photographer, Miss Daisy Stilwell, medical artist, and Mrs Hunt who was his clinical secretary. In 1941, Mr Frank Robinson also joined the Unit as a trainee.

An idea of what it was like in those early days of the war can be seen from the information provided by WH Wolstenholme of Sharston:

Baguley Plaque
Made by patients in appreciation of
Mr Moule (the figure on the left) and
Mr Bentley (the figure on the right).
The motto was SI VOS NOSE
MENDERAS MAXILLAE FRANCAS

"I joined the military in 1940, firstly visiting Dover Street where, as I was tall and fit, I was asked if I would join the Guards. I subsequently served in the Grenadier Guards doing guard duty at Windsor Castle. In 1942 I joined the 8th Army and took part in the invasion of Italy. I was wounded on 6th February 1943 and following treatment in the Dressing Station of the 59th Military Hospital, Naples, transferred by Hospital Ship to Southampton and thence by troop train and hospital buses to the hospital at Wythenshawe.

I was given a colostomy and woke up to many tubes, bandages and glass rods with bowel visible. Was looked after by Staff Nurse Smith and Nurse Cruckshank. When the colostomy was closed up a bed pan was put on the end of the bed.

The Plastic and Maxillo-Facial Unit consisted of three 30-bedded wards: one male, one female and one officers' ward. Initially, personnel from all three Services and prisoners-of-war were treated on the unit. In addition, civilian air-raid casualties from the bombing of Manchester and Liverpool were admitted for treatment. Shortly afterwards, naval casualties were transferred to the Haslar

Naval Hospital at Portsmouth and air force casualties to East Grinstead. Dr Converse and his team stayed on until 1942 when they returned home because the United States of America had entered the war. This left the unit temporarily with no plastic surgeon until Pere Gabarro, a Catalan refugee from the Spanish Civil War, arrived. The unit continued to expand and, in 1943, a separately designed Dental Unit and Dental Laboratory were added. A Photography Department was also established, initially under the charge of Mr Moule. Previously, patients had to be transferred to the sanatorium for their operations but, in 1943, two operating theatres were opened at the EMS

Dr Pere Gabarro, Plastic Surgeon

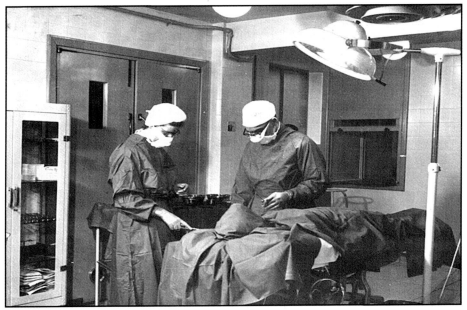

Operating Theatre

74

Hospital. After D-Day, large numbers of battle casualties were referred to the unit for treatment.

The last ambulance train was received in the early part of 1945 and the EMS Hospital closed except for the Plastic Surgery and Maxillo-Facial Unit. The Baguley site then reverted to its original purpose - provision of chest medicine.

In the period immediately after the war, servicemen with pulmonary tuberculosis were cared for within the Military Wing commanded by Major MM Nagley, Chest Physician, and staffed by the Royal Army Medical Corps and Queen Alexandra nurses, although it was under the administrative control of the senior officers of Baguley Sanatorium. The unit consisted of 128 beds for servicemen with pulmonary tuberculosis who were required to conform to the routine of the sanatorium.

In the late 1940s, there were some 550 beds provided for adult patients of both sexes. (In addition to the 302 beds available in the sanatorium, the Military Wing could accommodate up to 128 male cases.) Unfortunately, owing to nursing staff difficulties, the complement of beds in the sanatorium was reduced by approximately 120.

The sanatorium admitted patients in all stages of pulmonary tuberculosis. Other beds under the care of the Resident Surgical Officer were reserved for surgical cases admitted from neighbouring County Boroughs under the Co-ordinated Thoracic Surgery Scheme. Baguley Sanatorium was the centre of this scheme under the direction of Mr Graham Bryce.

Admissions in 1947 totalled 469 and, whilst all modern forms of therapy were used in suitable cases, routine sanatorium treatment remained the basis for all treatment. Consultant, pathological and physiotherapy services were fully provided. As well, there had been an efficient and productive Handicrafts Department, known as 'Baguley Crafts', for over twenty years. The Recreation Hall, which seated 400, contained a completely equipped stage, dressing rooms and cinema projectors. This hall was also used for religious services, the Chancel being recessed at the end opposite the stage behind roller shutters.

After the war, the Plastic Surgery and Maxillo-Facial Unit was run by Mr AHR Champion FRCS, Surgeon in Charge. Industrial and road injuries and burns made up the bulk of the admissions, although every effort was made to admit other patients who required plastic surgery or complicated maxillo-facial operations. The unit was not able to work to capacity for some years owing to the shortage of nursing staff. Even so, in 1947, 570 patients were admitted and 1,446 out-patients were seen. Patients of all ages were accommodated and were, at that time, in two pavilions (male and female) in the Emergency Hospital.

Left to right: Mr Alan Moule, a Ward Sister and Mr FH Bentley at Baguley Hospital in 1940

The Post-War Period

In 1946, following demobilisation from the army, Randell Champion joined the Plastic Surgery and Maxillo-Facial Unit at Baguley Hospital. Shortly afterwards, following the amnesty declaration after the Spanish Civil War, Mr Gabarro returned to Barcelona. Mr Andrew McDowall, following his war service in Italy, Germany and the Far East, subsequently joined the team. At that time, most of the plastic surgery was undertaken on the unit at the EMS Hospital at Wythenshawe, with some work at the Christie Hospital and some at the Duchess of York Hospital.

Mr Randell Champion

Mr Randell Champion, an Australian, first qualified in dental surgery and subsequently took the MB BS in Melbourne in 1935. He came to England and obtained the Diploma of DLO in 1938 and in the same year gained the Edinburgh Fellowship in Surgery. He underwent a course of training in plastic surgery at Rooksdown House under Sir Harold Gillies and was then posted with the rank of Major, Royal Army Medical Corps, as Surgeon in Charge of Number 1 Maxillo-Facial Unit in Alexandria. Here, he was responsible for the management of large numbers of severe facial injuries and all types of major soft tissue damage - in particular, extensive burns. He was mentioned in dispatches. Following his return to civilian life, he was appointed to the EMS Plastic and Jaw Unit at Leeds and later moved to Manchester in 1946 to become the first consultant in plastic surgery in Manchester when the National Health Service began in 1948. Under his enthusiastic and determined guidance, the unit began to treat increasing numbers of burns and major injuries as well as more facial cases and head and neck cancer. As a trainer of plastic surgeons, 'Champ' - as he was known on the unit - was fulsome in his praise of good work. He did not suffer fools gladly, however, and woebetide the trainee who did not realise the danger signals - the soft whistling under the breath or the skin on the back of the Chief's neck turning a puce colour. Champ's summoning of the theatre nursing staff back from a coffee break, by kicking on the dividing wall of the rest room, was thought to be a relic of his time in charge of the Maxillo-Facial Unit in the Middle East. His main interest lay in facial surgery - especially surgery for cleft lip and palate and carcinoma of the face. He wrote several papers on his experience gained at the Christie Hospital. He had the satisfaction of knowing that the unit, which started with some 50 beds at the time of his appointment in 1946, expanded to over 200 beds throughout the North West region.

In 1969, the unit was transferred to Withington Hospital into a purpose-adapted unit of 70 beds. There were male, female and children's wards and a self-contained Adult Burns Unit of 12 cubicles. This unit included a clinical bathing facility linked with an air-conditioned burns dressing theatre, an anaesthetic room, sterilising rooms and changing accommodation. This was the first time that the burns facility had been isolated from plastic surgery and it marked a significant step forward in the treatment of both types of patients.

Mr Frank Robinson qualified in medicine at the University of Manchester in 1940 and worked subsequently in the Plastic Surgery and Macillo-Facial Unit at Baguley EMS Hospital with Dr Pere Gabarro before being called up to the Army in 1944. He always spoke most highly of Gabarro's activity and obviously had learned a great deal from the work of this Spanish plastic surgeon. He had been most impressed with his meticulous operating skills and artistic approach. After the war, Robinson returned to the Manchester Royal Infirmary and undertook further surgical training with Mr Wilson Hey, Mr FH Bentley and Sir Harry Platt. After obtaining the Fellowship of the Royal College of Surgeons in 1949, he returned to the Plastic Surgery and Maxillo-Facial Unit at Baguley Hospital.

Mr Alan Weldon Moule was associated with the unit from its first origins at Baguley Hospital. In 1951, he transferred the Oral Surgery Department to Withington Hospital and the two units were reunited

Mr Frank Robinson, Plastic Surgeon

Alan Weldon Moule

subsequently at Withington Hospital in 1969. Over the years, Moule established an international reputation for his contributions to oral and maxillo-facial surgery. This pre-eminence was recognised by his election as President of the British Association of Oral Surgery in 1963 and by the award of the Down Medal, by the same Association in 1981 in recognition of his distinguished services to the specialty in this country. Despite this international reputation, Alan Moule was a very modest man and a delightful person to work with.

One of the longest serving members of the nursing team at Baguley was Miss Astbury, who joined the unit in the 1940s and was in charge of the burns dressing station until her retirement, just before the unit moved to Withington Hospital.

Initially, the dressings of burns centred around a saline bath in the Male Ward at Baguley which was heated by stoking a boiler outside the hut. Miss Astbury recalled that the bath was never very popular with the patients as the temperature of the bath was frequently less than tepid. In the late 1950s, a new burns dressing unit was built, following which the standard of care improved considerably despite the fact that the plastic surgery and burns patients were still being nursed alongside each other on the adult wards.

Probably the most renowned member of the nursing staff on the Unit was Jack Hales, who had sustained severe burns of the face and body whilst serving with the paratroops in the war. He received initial treatment at Rooksdown House and later at Leeds under the care of Mr Randell Champion. Randell had undertaken a most successful tube pedicle reconstruction of Jack Hales' badly scarred chin - a fact to which Champion not infrequently drew the attention of trainees at the end of a visit to the Male Ward on his rounds. Jack Hales was Charge Nurse on the Male Ward for 25 years up to his retirement and his time in the unit was characterised by the military precision with which he ran his

Miss Astbury receiving a presentation on her retirement.
Jack Hales is third from the left.

ward. Patients were 'listed' for dressings and a ceremonial procession with the dressing trolley was made to each bed: each patient was expected to respond suitably when his turn came and to exhibit no timidity at the thought of his dressing being changed. Mr Hales' contribution of long and splendid service to the unit was fittingly acknowledged by the award of the MBE in the New Year Honours List in the year in which he retired.

Baguley and Wythenshawe Hospitals
1950 - 1955

Wythenshawe Hospital was first discussed as an idea in July 1939 but, with war imminent, the priority was to adapt Baguley Sanatorium to handle the expected rush of casualties from air-raids. The debate about a new hospital was put 'on hold' throughout the war years and the immediate post-war period.

Baguley Sanatorium and Annex in 1947

After the war, many of the wards built at the beginning of the war remained disused and derelict whilst the future use of the buildings was considered.

In 1948, when the National Health Service began, the hospital was taken over by the South Manchester Hospital Management Committee. Nine of the 17 ward blocks stood empty: the huts were heated by coke stoves and the main hospital corridor was open to the elements on either side. The buildings stood in a field of rough grass. The austere post-war years hadn't helped matters either: ward windows were tied in place with bandages or string; ward doors were warped and would not close; roofs leaked, and, cash was scarce. By 1950, the last of the military patients had departed and one ward was renovated to be

Children's ENT Unit before renovation - note the coke fire chimney and metal beds

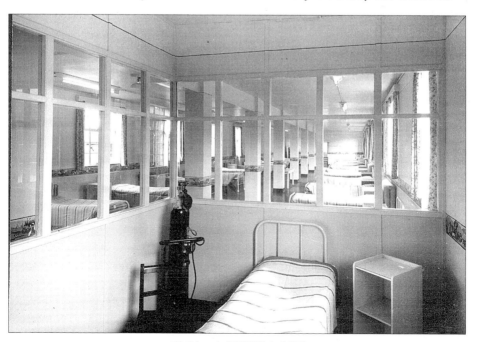

Children's ENT Unit-1950

Pathology Laboratory 1960

Children outside the Plastic Surgery Ward

used as a children's ward for the removal of tonsils and adenoids.

Manchester Regional Board wanted a general hospital. On 1st January 1952, therefore, an independent Wythenshawe Hospital was established, with Baguley remaining as a chest hospital. The Administration Officer was GC Chadwick and the Matron was Miss A Morgan (later Mrs Doolan). Its problems included derelict huts, unkempt grounds, and a shortage of cash and staff to deal with its 200 patients (including 75 from the Christie cancer hospital). The hospital was to serve the new Township of Wythenshawe and there were plans for 375 beds: 115 for men, 165 for women and 95 for children. To overcome the shortage of staff, the training of state registered nurses started at Baguley Sanatorium and state enrolled nurses at Wythenshawe Hospital.

Outside, the hospital looked like an army camp. Inside, patients lay on old hair mattresses on military iron bedsteads. On opening, the hospital comprised three Plastic Surgery wards (1 male, 1 female and 1 children). Two wards were loaned to Christie Hospital and Holt Radium Institute for patients requiring radium treatment. The Christie Hospital and Holt Radium Institute patients were later transferred back to Christie Hospital.

The local paper, *Wythenshawe Recorder*, recorded the changes being made to improve the hospital on 14 March 1952:

Wythenshawe Hospital is fast being brought up to the standard of a well-equipped modern general infirmary. With the opening of the new women's surgical department last Tuesday, there are now nine wards in use, and others will be put into operation when trained nursing staff becomes available.

The drab brick exterior of this network of single-storey buildings, which sprawls beside Baguley Hospital, conceals an interior bright with fresh paint and gay curtains. Steadily, workmen are moving along the long rows of wards installing fluorescent lighting and replacing combustion stoves with water radiators. All the wards are being decorated in various pastel shades and soon each will have its own reading room for patients able to get about.

The new surgical section, which can accommodate 25 patients, has been temporarily housed until the permanent ward has been completed renovated.

The opening of the new ward inspired rumours that old rusted beds, which had

Wythenshawe General Casualty Entrance

lain idle since the war, when the place was a service hospital, had been brought into use.

Said Mr C G Chadwick, the administrative officer, "Some of the beds are not new, but they were never in the wartime hospital. They have been borrowed from stock at Withington Hospital and have been sand-blasted and re-enamelled, so that they are now as good as new. All of them have been fitted with brand new spring mattresses."

Two geriatric wards were subsequently opened, but the building was not satisfactory: floors were concrete and the rain leaked in. Two empty wards were upgraded and the geriatric patients were transferred to these upgraded wards.

Miss Ann Morgan, Matron

Carpets bought with the proceeds of a concert held at Woodhouse Park Labour Club, were presented by Councillor Charles Hall to the matron of Wythenshawe Hospital, Miss A T Morgan, on Monday. The carpets are for the relaxation rooms at the hospital where patients can watch television, write letters or read books. In the picture (from left) are: Mr Alfred Morris (prospective Labour candidate for Wythenshawe), Councillor Hall, Miss E Fisher, Miss Morgan, Mr H Noden (Club secretary) and Mr A Smith (Club President).

Whilst all this was going on, Baguley Hospital continued to treat pulmonary tuberculosis. Dr Leslie Doyle describes the conditions at Baguley in a letter:

"I came to Baguley Hospital on 27 December 1950.

It was about this time that the designation was changed from Sanatorium to Hospital; it was devoted entirely to the medical and surgical treatment of Pulmonary Tuberculosis.

The hospital had about 400 beds. The staff comprised a (I) Medical

Superintendent, Dr Hugh George Trayer who held this position from the early 1920s. He served with the R.A.M.C. in Serbia during the 1914-18 war and received an award from the Serbian Government; (II) a Deputy Superintendent (Senior Hospital Medical Officer), Dr Rob Sinton; several doctors in junior posts. I was appointed a Junior Registrar (£650 per year). There were three consultant Thoracic Surgeons; Mr Arthur Graham-Bryce, Mr James Glennie and Mr Frank Nicholson. The pathology services were run from Withington Hospital (Dr L Stent). In a small laboratory on site, blood counts and some biochemical and bacteriological investigations were carried out. (Mr Evan Betts was the technician in charge).

Dr Leslie Doyle

Dr Kathleen Lodge succeeded Dr Stent in 1954 and was the first full time Consultant Pathologist on the site. She later became Chairman of the Medical Executive Committee and played a major role in planning the new hospital.

Although this was an era when the first antibiotic and chemotherapy drugs were being introduced, the long established practices of bed rest and fresh air were still the order of the day. The extent of bed rest varied according to the extent of the tuberculous disease and the severity of the constitutional symptoms such as, weight loss and fever. In advanced cases, absolute bed rest was practiced: permanently in bed and fed by a nurse. All patients had two periods each day of one hour's complete rest, each period, in bed.

The streptomycin and P.A.S (Para-Amino-Salicylic) had been recently introduced; but the dosage and length of treatment varied greatly from hospital to hospital. Large doses of these drugs were complicated by skin rashes, fever and in the case of streptomycin, 8th nerve damage (deafness).

In the early 1950s a national trial involving many centres in Britain, including Baguley Hospital, was set up to evaluate this treatment and a further drug, isonizian, introduced about 1952. The trial lasted about 5 years.

The standard major surgical treatment for pulmonary tuberculosis was a thoracoplasty, a mutilating operation, usually carried out in two or more stages; varying portions of the upper ribs on one side were removed, this enabled the chest wall to fall in and reduce the size and movement of the upper lobe. The cases for thoracoplasty were carefully selected. Even without chemotherapy, the results were surprisingly good.

In the early and mid-1950s, local resections of lung and lobectomy were being carried out - the chemotherapy (streptomycin, and P.A.S.) was prescribed as a 'cooling off' pre-operative measure. In Baguley Hospital, one young woman with localised, cavitating tuberculous disease in one upper lobe, had the usual 3 months 'cooling off' chemotherapy; but her operation was delayed for over 6 months, for non-medical reasons, with continuation of the chemotherapy. When the upper lobe was finally resected the cavity was firmly closed and there was no evidence of residual tuberculous disease present.

This was the first case at Baguley Hospital where the efficacy of long-term chemotherapy was clearly demonstrated. The national trial, later, amply confirmed the result of this young woman's treatment, in many more cases.

In the early 1950s, the hospital discipline was strict: Visiting was allowed on Saturday and Sunday afternoons, for one hour, and for half an hour, on Wednesday evenings. On these occasions, before the appointed time for opening of the large hospital gates, a large number of visitors waited patiently. On opening the gates there was a rush of people making for the wards. The vast majority of visitors came by bus to the hospital gates.

Corridor to Admininistration Offices

89

In these early 1950 years, the administrative staff was small. The Chief Administrator (Hospital Steward) was Mr Robert Lawton Hall; he was well-remembered man who had served in The Cheshire Regiment in World War I. He won a MM and a DSM. As well as looking after hospital maintenance, he paid the hospital staff each Thursday and gave monthly reports to the House Committee. His secretary, Miss Meredith (an elderly lady), was the sister of Billy Meredith, a famous Welsh footballer who played for several clubs in the Manchester area.

Mr Hall ran the hospital piggery situated not far from one of the wards. He reared his pigs in well-constructed sties. Their sale gave money to Manchester Corporation. The pigs were the breed, Large White, and one sow was called "Baguley Lady". Mr Hall conducted the delivery of a farrow and gave this a priority. He was often assisted by members of the medical staff.

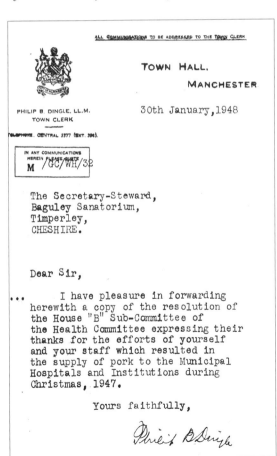

ALL COMMUNICATIONS TO BE ADDRESSED TO THE TOWN CLERK

TOWN HALL,

MANCHESTER

PHILIP B. DINGLE, LL.M.
TOWN CLERK

TELEPHONE. CENTRAL 3377 (EXT. 394).

30th January,1948

IN ANY COMMUNICATIONS
HEREIN PLEASE QUOTE

M /GC/WH/32

The Secretary-Steward,
Baguley Sanatorium,
Timperley,
CHESHIRE.

Dear Sir,

I have pleasure in forwarding
herewith a copy of the resolution of
the House "B" Sub-Committee of
the Health Committee expressing their
thanks for the efforts of yourself
and your staff which resulted in
the supply of pork to the Municipal
Hospitals and Institutions during
Christmas, 1947.

Yours faithfully,

Philip B Dingle

The Obiturary of Mr Robert Lawton Hall

Born in Whitefield, Lancashire, Mr Hall had served in many local hospitals during a lifelong career as a hospital secretary. He was, for 19 years, at the District Infirmary, Ashton-under-Lyne, and finally, for 32 years, at Baguley Sanatorium where he was secretary-steward.

During World War II, his service also centred round the Baguley Emergency Medical Service. Mr Hall was a Fellow of the Institute of Hospital Administrators.

In World War I, Mr Hall was awarded the DCM and the MM during service with the 6th Battalion, The Cheshire Regiment. He also served in German East Africa and the King's African Rifles and later in the war was transferred to the Machine Gun Corps. He was a former chairman of the now disbanded Machine Gun Corps Old Comrades' Association.

The length of stay in hospital varied from 6 months to 20 years. Some of the latter group had advanced amyloidosis - common and well described in the nineteenth century.

With the sexes separated, the up-patients had their meals in the large dining hall. Great efforts were made to overcome the patients' boredom from a long stay in hospital. The recreation hall was regularly used for visits by choirs, amateur dramatics groups, cinema shows and whist drives. Other diversions for patients were woodwork for men, needlework for women and painting for both, run by experienced artisans.

Other features of hospital activity were:

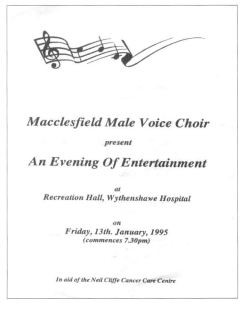

Macclesfield Male Voice Choir

present

An Evening Of Entertainment

at
Recreation Hall, Wythenshawe Hospital

on
Friday, 13th. January, 1995
(commences 7.30pm)

In aid of the Neil Cliffe Cancer Care Centre

The recreation hall referred to in Dr Doyle's letter was still in use up to recent times as shown in the programme above.

1   A fine bowling green in the hospital grounds for patients' use.

2.   A large vegetable garden, comprising several sites, which employed several men who used a large farm cart and horse called 'Blossom'.

3   An extensive nursery with several greenhouses to supply flowers and shrubs for hospital flower beds. The flower beds of Baguley Hospital were a well-known local feature.

A new chest clinic at Baguley Hospital was opened at the end of November 1952 by the Lord Mayor of Manchester, Alderman Douglas Gosling. On this occasion, Councillor Eveline Hill MP summarised: "It is very right that the local authorities should take a real interest in the work of hospitals, for so much good work is done by them. A few years ago there seemed little hope of the time when we could open a new hospital service."

"Now we have a clinic which will be of great use indeed. Here we have in Wythenshawe a very large township. A large number of people need the clinic's service - among them are people who have become TB patients because they once lived in congested parts of the city. This clinic will help considerably towards restoring them to health."

The Lord Mayor added: "One wonders how many people in Wythenshawe have chest trouble as a result of living in the city's crowded areas for so long. Here, indeed, you now have wonderful equipment which must give every patient encouragement." He went on to pinpoint a major difficulty - the lack of nurses in this important branch of medicine, leading to 100 beds empty beds. The Lord

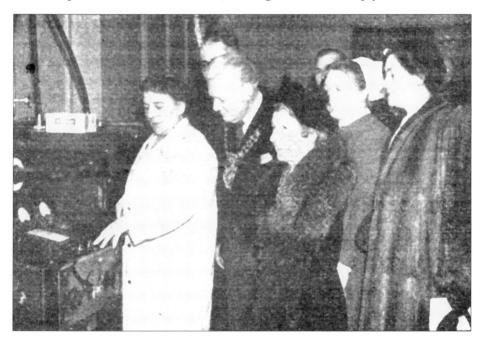

Lord Mayor examines new X-ray machine

Miss M E Cowell, radiographer to the new clinic and to Baguley Hospital, explains the workings of an X-ray machine, part of the equipment which will ease pressure on central Manchester chest clinic and provide a local out patients' service for Wythenshawe people suffering from chest complaints. Looking on are the Lord Mayor (Alderman Douglas Gosling), the Lady Mayoress, Miss N H Burrows (Matron of Baguley Hospital) and Mrs Eveline Hill, MP.

Mayor stressed: "We do want a strong nation. From what I have seen this afternoon I wish this place was treble the size." (Matron Burrows estimated that 40 nurses were needed immediately - at least 20 of them with training.)

Dr HG Trayer, Physician Superintendent and Chairman of the Baguley Hospital Medical Advisory Committee, reminded the assembled that, in 1949, 20,000 tuberculosis patients died. In 1950, the number of victims was down to 16,000, although known cases in that period had actually increased by 12,000. Whereas only a few years before five people had died from the disease every four days, the toll in 1952 was less that one a day.

"But we can do better than that." said Dr Trayer, "One day we hope that treatment will not be necessary because then there will be no one to treat. "Fundamentally the needs are for rest and diet - the same two elements as were needed 50 years ago. But how many rest in this restless world?" Dr Trayer agreed with the Lord Mayor when he said that it was no longer a case of getting the disease and giving up hope.

Patients' waiting room - Out-patients Department

94

The chest clinic, which opened two days a week, served as the out-patient department of the hospital and provided services for the diagnosis and treatment of diseases of the chest - especially pulmonary tuberculosis.

Consultants from Baguley Hospital and the Oxford Road Clinic staffed the clinic which was housed in a building which accommodated the Civil Nursing Reserve in 1940. It was converted and equipped at a cost of £4,927.

The clinic accommodation comprised a reception room, general offices, Almoners' office, two consulting rooms, two patients' reception and dressing rooms (male and female), X-ray room, and staff and doctors' rest rooms.

Medical staff - December 1957
Back Row: Satya Chatterjee, Leslie Doyle, Ian Cathhill, Seamus O'Daley,
Kevin Murphy,
Front Row: Miss Herbert, Derek Turnbull, Tom Wilson, Peter Jones and
Margaret Gardiner

By the mid 1950s, Wythenshawe Hospital was becoming known as a 'friendly' hospital. The *Wythenshawe Recorder* of 4th May 1956 reported:

"Wythenshawe must be one of the most un-hospital like hospitals in Manchester, possibly in the whole North of England.

White wooden gates have replaced the more usual high wrought iron entrances which tend to give many people a penned-in feeling. Lawns border the drive. The hospital bears little resemblance to a hospital. Not quite home to home, but nearer than might be expected.

It is not merely appearances, though, which have gained Wythenshawe Hospital a country-wide reputation for friendliness.

A little unorthodoxy lies behind it, a departure from convention. Patients say so. Staff say so. Everyone says so. There is an easy-going relationship between patients and the staff in white. A relaxed atmosphere is encouraged and effected without detriment.

"We want people to get better in as pleasant surroundings and conditions as possible." explained Mr James Lionel Pugh, Administrative Officer. As a general Hospital serving a 90,000-strong township, Wythenshawe Hospital only came into its own a short time ago. And the fact that it may soon be replaced by a new one is not retarding development or progress.

Going back to 1940, the war was well under way and Manchester had become a target for the German bombers. Heavy air-raid casualties were feared. An emergency hospital in the outskirts was needed because chances were that the city hospitals might not have been able to cope.

Fortunately, its capacity as an emergency hospital was never tested. Air-raid casualties did not fill its wards. Instead there were casualties of another kind - men from the front lines and the Hospital was taken over by the military. Men who had been in blown-up tanks, men horribly burned were flown back to this country and moved out to Wythenshawe.

The emphasis then was on plastic surgery. People were given new faces, new lives. Futures, of which many must have despaired, were re-moulded under the skilful guidance of specialists, doctors and nurses.

Against this macabre setting the spirit of friendliness grew.

Social Club - Wythenshawe Hospital

"Things were very austere but there was a wonderful atmosphere," recalled Miss Edith Gibbon, Senior Medical Photographer.

Towards the end of the war, more of the beds were being allocated to civilians. But the military lingered on until 1952.

Head porter, Mr Patrick Hanely, who had been at the Hospital since 1941, has noted the changes which have taken place. "All of them have been for the better." he said.

In the early days, for instance, each of the wards was heated by two coke-burning stoves-stoked more often than not by the military! - situated in the middle with chimneys going out through the centre of the ward roof.

Needless to say, the last of these have now disappeared to be replaced by a central heating system throughout the hospital.

Today in each ward there is a TV set, provided by a voluntary subscription. And a popular feature too, especially with the children. "We've almost had to

rearrange ward methods so that the youngsters can watch Children's Hour."
laughed Mr Pugh.

At the moment the TVs are providing Mr Pugh with rather a headache. All the
sets need converting to ITV and the big problem is finding the £150 required to
convert them.

Possibly this may come within the scope of the recently formed League of
Friends for Wythenshawe and Baguley hospitals.

Quite apart from raising money, though, the League helps to form a closer link
between the people of Wythenshawe and the two hospitals. League members
have taken over the visiting of patients since their formation.

Included in their calls are the two children's wards in Wythenshawe Hospital.
Incidentally, being in hospital does not give children chance to skip their

Sister Helen Gribbin joining in the game with Michael Burney (11), Robert Shackle
(5), Fred Clough (12) at the wicket, and Peter Rattigan (7)

Physiotherapist conducting an exercise class

lessons. *Two teachers are on the spot to take classes morning and afternoon in the wards.*

The interior of Wythenshawe Hospital is decorated nearly completely throughout in bright, contemporary style. All the wards lie of a main, lengthy, glassed-in corridor.

No visitor could fail to notice the homeliness of the hospital and the cheerful ease of the patients. One old lady said to Mr Pugh as he showed her round the day room in a ward: "Thinking of buying it? It's worth anybody's money!"

Wythenshawe is one of the few hospitals with an extensively equipped medical photographic department. Anything from a person to a microbe can be photographed.

A sidelight on this department's work is the entertainment of patients Regular film shows are given. Solely for the staff is a social club in the hospital grounds. It sports a bar and has facilities for dances, concerts and most indoor sports. It is not difficult to see how friendliness is fostered."

Radio Baguley

Early in 1959, Radio Baguley arrived at Baguley Hospital. This was recorded in an article from one of the local papers dated 23rd July:

Calling all patients at Radio Baguley

A broadcasting station in miniature, with a staff of eight drawn from all walks of life - in Manchester's Baguley Hospital!

Visiting a friend there I heard part of the twice-weekly record request programme and "show" delivered in the modern manner by the patients for the patients. Here's one instance of the slickness.

A record by Cliff Richard entitled "Move It" was not available and scriptwriter-compere Bert Thorpe cracked: "Sorry, it really has been moved. You will have to satisfied with 'I'll be Satisfied'"

Before Mr Thorpe took on the job he "did not know the difference between Marty Wilde and Mantovani". Now he talks glibly about recording artists and he and his fellow-workers are delighting the patients in the two 1 1/2 hour broadcasts over the hospital's private network on Sunday mornings and Wednesday afternoons.

The biggest problem is the shortage of new records. Every source of charitable supply is tapped. Some are bought by the group themselves and Mr Thorpe says: "The pops are the tops with our listeners."

Others in this wonderful group are: Pauline Gilbert (19), a clerk who acts as secretary; Ann Massey (18), a shop assistant who is an announcer. Mary Glover (32), the treasurer, will gladly give up her duties on August 1 after six years in hospital.

In charge of the turntable is Terry Sweeney, who comes from Broughton, Salford.

Former grocer's assistant Allan Gittins, a Wythenshawe man, is co-producer and compere, while Bill Crowther is the librarian. Petite Pat Lavin, aged 20, and a bride of 12 weeks, helps "in all departments."

Bert Thorpe, with Anne Massey (left) and Mary Glover (right), keeping the entertainment rolling in Baguley Hospital's own broadcasting station

The "staff" changes frequently - happy thought! - but rather reluctantly. Mr Thorpe and Miss Massey will both be making their final farewell broadcasts early next month.

If you have any modern records to spare send them along to Baguley. They really can make use of them.

(The above newspaper article was given to the author by a patient, Norma Millar of Timperley.)

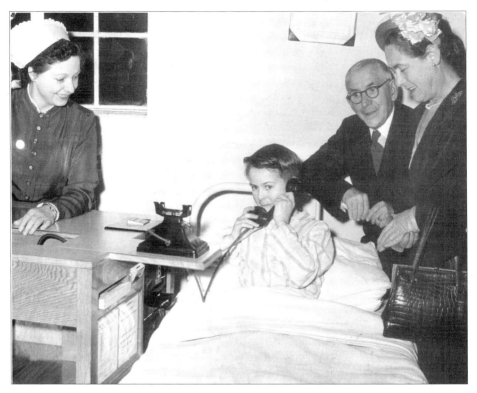

David Norbury using the telephone in 1957

Mobile pay-phones provided by the hospital charities became available for use by patients by the mid 1950s.

The New Hospital

In July 1955, aware of Wythenshawe's need for a completely new hospital, the Ministry of Health included Wythenshawe in its list of the first new hospitals to be built under the National Health Service. The plan was to build on the site of the Baguley Emergency Hospital, starting with a maternity hospital. JL Pugh was appointed as the first full-time administrator. Temporarily, the hutted hospital had to do, with the main corridor covered in.

Years of negotiations and argument between Manchester Regional Hospital Board, Manchester Corporation and Central Government then followed. The proposed siting of the hospital and the type of fuel to be used for heating were the issues of contention.

The original plan, proposed by the Ministry of Health and announced through the Manchester Regional Hospital Board, called for the demolition of the hutted hospital and the building of a new 516-bed hospital on the same site.

Matron, Miss A T Morgan, gets a welcome from three year old Terence Todd

The Regional Hospital Board appointed a Sub-Committee to build the hospital. One of the prime movers of both the Board and the Sub-Committee was Alderman RE Thomas.

In due course, the Sub-Committee appointed architects to design the hospital. The site was surveyed, the land tested and the plans for the number of beds for each speciality were discussed with the medical staff.

Most of the land required for building the hospital on the site of the then Wythenshawe Hospital belonged to

Withenshawe's £2.5 million general hospital - as originally planned

Manchester Corporation. In January 1958, the Regional Hospital Board asked the Corporation to sell the land to them or grant them a long term lease. In March 1958, the Hospital Board wrote to the Corporation informing them that it proposed burning coal at the new hospital.

The Corporation replied that they were willing to lease the land to the Hospital Board, provided that the Hospital Board would conform to the Corporation's clean air policy. The Corporation indicated that it expected public buildings to use gas or electricity for the purpose of heating. The Engineer of the Hospital Board was invited to meet the Smoke Inspectors employed by Manchester Corporation in order to discuss the heating problem but there was no reply from the Regional Board to this suggestion.

In April 1959, the Wythenshawe Sub-Committee of the Hospital Board decided to scrap the existing plans and start afresh, with new plans for a hospital on the land owned by the Hospital Board in the grounds of Baguley Hospital. The reason given for this change of plan was Manchester Corporation's refusal to allow oil or coal-fired heating.

The new plan called for the demolition of the 105 beds and and the building of a 350-bed hospital. Under the new plan, the hutted hospital would be retained

Sir Robert Thomas
Lord Mayor of Manchester 1962
and Freeman of the City of Manchester

to accommodate what were known as 'Chronic Sick' - the large majority of whom were elderly people too ill to look after themselves.

On the 24 June 1960, the Hospital Board and the architects explained the new plan to the local Hospital Committee. Alderman Thomas and other committee members protested that the architects had completely failed to take account of the needs of the users of the hospital. They had placed the main entrance on Floats Road - at the furthest possible point from any house in Wythenshawe, or any bus service in Wythenshawe, excepting the hourly 44 service.

Under the old plan, the entrance would have been on the Southmoor Road extension close to the junction of the Hollyhedge Road extension and convenient for the frequent 101 service.

Model of new hospital

105

Main Corridor - 1956

At the next meeting of the Sub-Committee, Alderman Thomas tried to get the Hospital Board to revert to the original plan without success. Arrangements were then made through Will Griffiths MP for a meeting on 28th July 1960 with the Minister of Health, Mr Derek Walker Smith. Unfortunately, the Minister resigned before the proposed meeting and the meeting was held with the Parliamentary Private Secretary to the Minister of Health, Miss Edith Pitt, MP.

The main points raised by the Sub-Committee at this meeting were:

1. That the entrance to the new hospital was being sited at the furthest possible point from the buses and houses of Wythenshawe.

2. That, whereas the old plan would demolish the wooden huts built in 1940 to last 10 years, the new plan would demolish comparatively good wards at the Baguley Hospital.

3. That Wythenshawe was being declared a smokeless zone, yet the Minister of Health was proposing to burn coal in the new hospital.

4. That the Corporation had never been asked to consider oil as a fuel for the new hospital and had always been willing to do so if the request had been made.

5. That the plans for the old site were far more advanced than the plans for the new site and, consequently, the new hospital could be built more quickly on the old site than on the new one.

Site plan of new hospital

In view of all these circumstances, the Minister was asked to consider reverting to the original site. The protest was rejected by the new Minister of Health, Mr Enoch Powell, on the grounds that any reversion to the original site would involve a considerable delay. He decided that the new hospital would be built on land north of Baguley Hospital, with a new approach road from Southmoor Road on the north side and the Maternity entrance on the south side.

The *Manchester Guardian* of Thursday 26th January 1961 carried the following report:

Wythenshawe in New Hospitals List

29 Major schemes for 1964-5

The second phase of the new Wythenshawe Hospital in Manchester is among 29 major hospital building schemes which the Minister of Health, Mr Enoch Powell, has chosen for starting by 1964-5.

The list contains six new hospitals, one of them for mentally subnormal patients, and the development or modernisation of 23 others. Hospital boards will be expected to complete the planning so that building can be begun not later than 1964-5. This is the first time that a provisional time limit for starting a hospital scheme has been included in the announcement of selected projects.

Mr Powell, who published the list of projects and the starting time in a written Parliamentary answer yesterday, also stated that the provisional figure for capital expenditure on hospitals in 1962-63, subject to the economic situation, would be £36 millions, compared with £31 millions in 1961-62.

Without offering firm commitments, Mr Powell has given regional hospital boards tentative planning limits based on a capital expenditure rising to about £50 millions by 1965-66. Boards have been asked to prepare proposals for subsequent years on an estimate of what is needed and practicable.

Free limit raised

The Minister has raised from £30,000 to £60,000 the maximum cost of individual projects which hospital boards can undertake without his prior authority. The first of a series of building notes on hospital planning and the design of departments was published on Monday. Others will follow rapidly.

"These and an associated system of cost limits (Mr Powell stated) will simplify and expedite the planning of schemes by boards and their

examination and approval by me. In future when a scheme is approved in principle, a starting date will be given so that hospital boards will be able to carry through the planning and execution in the knowledge that the project will not subsequently be held up."

The Minister has asked boards to complete the planning of a number of major additional schemes: new general hospitals at Basildon, Stevenage, and Abergavenny, a long stay geriatric hospital at Pontypridd, the first phase of a new hospital at Exeter, and the second phase of the new Wythenshawe Hospital.

Six years late, building of the Maternity Hospital began. It was the first phase of major extension to Wythenshawe Hospital. On 18th October 1965, with a marque on the old Baguley bowling green, the new Wythenshawe Maternity Hospital, built at a cost of £720,000, was opened by the Minister of Health, Mr Kenneth Robinson.

There were three L-shaped wards providing 60 lying-in and 20 ante-natal beds together with ten special care cots. The lying-in beds were situated on the ground and first floors, with the ante-natal beds on the top floor. Also on the top floor were the special care cots with an adjacent central milk preparation unit.

The two post-natal wards each had five four-bed rooms, 10 single rooms, day space and four nurseries, though babies were allowed to 'room-in' where desirable. All patients had built-in wardrobes, intercom, radio and an overbed table complete with vanity box and mirror. Added attractions were the sheltered gardens visible from most beds and an open roof where patients could relax when the Manchester weather allowed.

An integral part of the ground floor was the ante-natal clinic which had its own entrance and six examination rooms, each served by two changing cubicles. The examination rooms were linked on their other side by a 'working corridor'. A buffet and a play space for children was included in the spacious reception area. Another useful feature was a room for lectures and ante-natal exercises for expectant mothers.

It was said at the time that the designer's aim was to create a group of buildings which were welcoming in appearance and domestic in scale without imparing functional efficiency. To quote from the brochure issued for the opening

Kenneth Robinson MP at the opening ceremony

ceremony - "We believe they have succeeded and that the building will be a distinct amenity in both looks and service. The clean, strong lines of the facade have grown from a desire 'to combine a generous window area with privacy and protection from excessive sunlight.' This has been achieved by overhanging roofs and balconies and, in the wards, by horizontal and vertical baffles which are incorporated in the windows themselves."

The *Architects Journal,* dated 30th March 1966, contained the following appraisal of the new unit:

The hospital is situated almost due south of Manchester on the eastern edge of a green belt. To the east is the largest part of the catchment area, the corporation housing estate of Wythenshawe with a population of 104,000. Other districts within the catchment area are Cheadle, Heald Green, Gatley, Hale, Altrincham and parts of Sale.

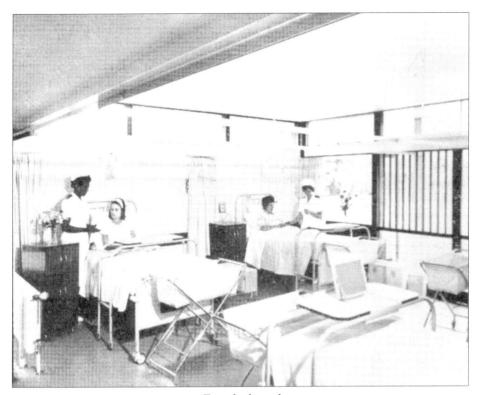
Four-bed ward

With the completion of the Maternity Unit - which is now regarded as one of the finest examples of hospital architecture of the period - work began in December 1965 on the main phase of Wythenshawe Hospital's development.

Dr Cliff Franklin, who began duties in September 1965 as a consultant at Baguley Hospital, was responsible for developing an anaesthesia service to support what was to become one of the leading cardio-thoracic surgical units in the United Kingdom. His pioneering work included establishing the role of anaesthetists in intensive care. In this, he collaborated with Dr Tom Wilson, Physician Superintendent at Baguley Hospital, and Dr John Breed who led the development of heart lung bypass for open heart surgery.

In 1965, only one open heart operation was carried out each week. These operations took place on Wednesdays, expertly co-ordinated by Mrs Lomax, Operating Theatre Superintendent. Each operation took up the complete day and, when things didn't go well, they ran late into the evening. They were then

Maternity staff
Front row, front left, Deborah Hickling (2nd), Mr Martin (4th), Kate Leigh (5th), Dr
Geffrey Feldman (6th), Miss Pearl Walker (7th), Mrs A Feldman(8th), Sister Jackson
(9th) and Mr Geffrey Morewood (10th).

followed by a long vigil in the Intensive Care Unit - in those days housed on Ward B3 East linked by a corridor to the operating theatre. These operations were carried out almost exclusively by Mr Gordon Jack and Mr John Dark. At that time, Mr Henri Moussalli was the registrar and Mr Fitzgerald the senior registrar. They were ably assisted by senior house officers, all of whom were from overseas with invariably one from Warsaw in Poland. The operating theatre monitoring equipment for open heart surgery - by present day standards a very 'Heath Robinson' array of instruments (but state-of-the-art at that time) - was overseen by Dr Maurice Bier, who spent almost as much of his time keeping the recording devices in an operational state as he spent noting the display of physiological changes in the patient. Disposable oxygenators were not available in Manchester at that time, which meant both John Breed and Cliff Franklin spent many 'happy' hours assembling the heart lung machines before use on the day of surgery and stripping them down afterwards to prepare them for autoclaving before re-use the following week. By 1965, the preparation of heart lung machines was by immersion in a large stainless steel tank containing fuming nitric acid in order to remove protein deposits. The acid remaining on the inner surfaces was then neutralised by rinsing with caustic soda before the equipment was autoclaved. This ritual was, prior to 1965, undertaken in the disused garage still standing on the east side of the link corridor between B3 East and Baguley Theatre. Subsequently, it was done within the Baguley Theatre Suite. Also, because the internal circuitry of the mechanical lung ventilators used at that time could not be removed for sterilisation before re-use on another patient, fumigation of this equipment (carried out in a side room on the Intensive Care Unit with the help of the then Charge Nurse, David Wilson) was a very important part of the ritual associated with intensive care.

Dr Cliff Franklin
outside Baguley Theatre Link
Corridor in 1969

The Intensive Care Unit in 1965 was presided over by Sister Kassabeer, who co-ordinated the work of the unit with a thoroughness second to none. The electronic equipment on the Intensive Care Unit included a number of cannibalised ex-War Department oscilloscopes used as heart monitors which, together with sphygmomanometers and clinical observation, formed the basis of monitoring critically ill patients. Blood gas analysis, which was a much more laborious procedure than it is nowadays, was carried out by the lung function staff in a laboratory run by Dr Satya Chatterjee.

In May 1969, the Plastic Surgery and Maxillo-Facial Unit and Wards W11, W13 and W15 were transferred to Withington Hospital.

The Wythenshawe and North Cheshire Hospital Management Committee which ran the new hospital comprised:

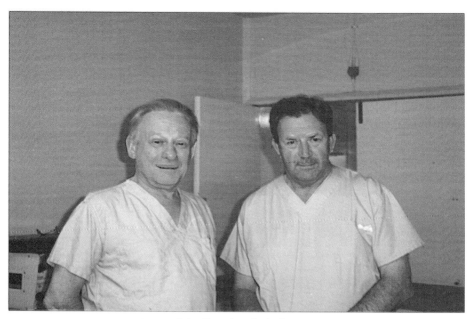

John Breed with Author

EK Willing-Denton, Esq JP OBE MA *(Chairman)*
E Fowden Esq FHA ARSH, Group Secretary
AG Pearson Esq FHA, Treasurer

Mrs TR Atherton	Dr RC Jennings
A Ball Esq	Dr KV Lodge
Councillor K Collins	TW Mercer Esq
Frank Gibson Esq	Major J Rubin
Dr B Gold	Dr JK Walley MA PhD
Mrs HM Hodgson	Dr TM Wilson
Councillor Mrs EM Hoyle JP CC	
A Yates Esq LL B	

At the end of the 1960s, Wythenshawe and North Cheshire Hospital became a general hospital and staff specialities were appointed as follows:

BAGULEY HOSPITAL

CHEST CLINIC	Dr SS Chatterjee
RESPIRATORY DISEASES	Dr L Doyle
	Dr TM Wilson
CARDIOLOGY	Dr C Bray

CARDIO-THORACIC SURGERY	Mr JF Dark
	Mr WK Douglas
	Mr MD Fitzgerald
	Mr GD Jack

WYTHENSHAWE MATERNITY HOSPITAL

ANTE-NATAL CLINIC	}	Mr RH Martin
POST-NATAL CLINIC	}	Miss PA Walker

WYTHENSHAWE HOSPITAL

GENERAL MEDICINE	Dr S Deen Mohamed
	Dr CDR Pengelly
	Dr GS Thompson
	Dr JS Parkinson
GENERAL SURGERY	Mr RP Davies
	Mr N MacDonald
ORTHOPAEDIC	Mr JD Evans
	Mr OO Cowpe
GYNAECOLOGY	Mr RH Martin
	Miss PA Walker
DERMATOLOGY	Dr M Garretts
EAR, NOSE AND THROAT	Mr WY Nasser
	Mr W Paterson
CEREBRAL PALSY	Dr B Epstein
PAEDIATRIC	Dr GV Feldman
	Dr D Macaulay
PAEDIATRIC SURGERY	Mr SJ Cohen
PLASTIC SURGERY	Mr RDP Craig

Gradually, bit by bit, the new hospital was built and commissioned by an enthusiastic group of doctors and nurses. The official opening by Princess Margaret took place on 11th July 1973, 21 years after the wartime huts became known as Wythenshawe Hospital.

Wythenshawe was Manchester's first wholly new general hospital. It had cost a total of £7.2 million.

Children outside the Plastic Surgery Ward

The publicity at the opening gave the following account:

'It combines a pleasing environment with good design and the most modern medical facilities. Special attention has been paid to landscaping and advantage has been taken of the sloping site so that patients at different ward levels can look out on to the gardens.

Alongside the main entrance is an ornamental pool. The hospital, with its 352 new beds, serves as a district general hospital for the Altrincham and Sale area as well as Wythenshawe. But with the three other hospitals already on the site - Baguley, the old Wythenshawe Hospital and the new Wythenshawe Maternity Hospital - upwards of 1,000 beds are available for treatment in a wide range of specialties.

A covered corridor links the new complex with the maternity hospital. In-patients enjoy a high standard of comfort and amenity. The general wards consist entirely of four-bedded and single rooms - the single rooms providing a

Princess Margaret at the Official Opening - 11th July 1973

Main entrance with pool

quarter of the total number of beds. The four-bed rooms have bed curtains for privacy and all patients have a built-in wardrobe.

Each ward has a large, pleasant day room with television. There are showers and baths too, and ward treatment rooms offer greater privacy for patients having dressings or minor treatment.

Food is, of course, always an important factor. At Wythenshawe a quick, efficient, up-to-date centralised tray service provides meals and a choice of menu.

Four general theatres, twice the original number, have been built and *are expected to speed up the reduction of waiting lists. A recovery room, where patients can receive more direct care after operations, forms part of the ultra-modern suite. A new operating theatre suite has also been provided for ear, nose and throat patients.*

Day Room with television

The large children's ward in the hospital is so arranged that adolescents can be accommodated separately from younger children. There are also eight rooms where mothers can 'room in' with their children - a situation that is often desirable with very young patients.

The Children's Department has its own entrance and out-patients' department ... away from the hurly-burly of the main department.

Outside view of general wards in 1974

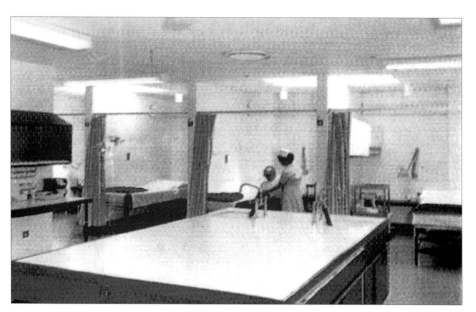

Casualty Department

At the presentation of an Engstrum Respirator are Tom Wilson, David Wilson, Dr Frank Wraith, Mrs Sheila McBride, George Parvell and Cliff Franklin. The ventilator was presented in 1970 to the Intensive Care Unit in memory of Dr Billy McBride.

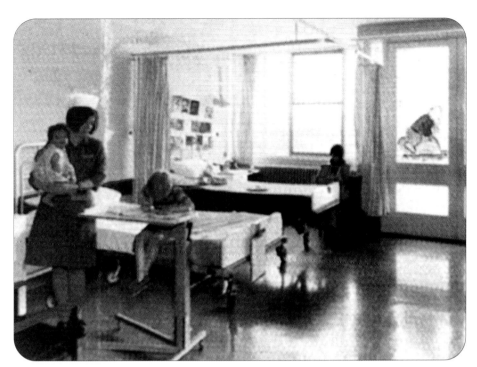

Children's Ward

In the Physical Medicine Department a large gymnasium and hydrotherapy pool provide excellent facilities for physiotherapy.

The very large Accident and Emergency Department, complete with operating theatres, is equipped to take major accidents. Adjacent is a five-day ward where patients undergoing intermediate surgical treatment can be nursed.

While the rest of the hospital provides the normal medical services, surgery, medicine, orthopaedics, gynaecology, E.N.T. surgery - the Cardio-Thoracic Department offers a highly-specialised service on a far wider, sub-regional basis.

Not only will the beds for the treatment of chest diseases - hitherto at Baguley Hospital - be continued, but there will be a greatly expanded programme of open-heart and other chest surgery.

For this work a very large, comprehensive department has been designed,

Physiotherapy Department

incorporating three operating theatres, a 12-bed intensive care unit, a cardiology unit and a lung function investigation unit.

A 'bedside computer' system, the first of its kind to be used in Britain, has been installed to give immediate information about patients in the intensive care unit.

Patient data can be fed into the system through any one of 36 keyboards located in laboratories, operating theatres, at patients' bedsides and in administrative and supervisory positions. It is expected that the department will be in the forefront in the use of advanced techniques.

A number of rooms at the hospital have been set aside so that relatives of seriously ill patients can stay overnight.

The hospital also has a shop and a bank, and there are facilities for recreation such as badminton and tennis.

Wythenshawe will participate in the Manchester Medical School's expanding undergraduate teaching activities and, of course, there are greatly increased opportunities for employment. Abundant accommodation is offered in modern hostels.

A modern training school and excellent tuition is available for nurses studying for the certificates of State Registration and State Enrolment. And trained nurses who wish to return to nursing will have the opportunity to take refresher courses at the Hospital.

A year after the opening of the new hospital, a covered walkway was built to link the new F wards with the old EMS huts.

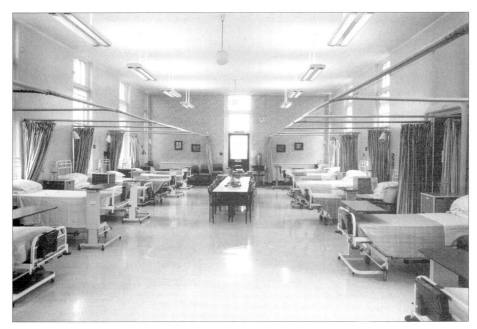

Ward B4

Wythenshawe Hospital had now become the most up-to-date hospital in the area, equipped with all the latest technology to serve the rapidly expanding population of South Manchester. Its 352 beds were allocated as follows:

General Surgery	64	General Medicine	24
Cardiology	8	Gynaecology	32
Orthopaedic/Traumatic	64	Cardio-Thoracic	22
Coronary Care	10	Children	60
Ear, Nose & Throat	40	5-day & Observation	16
Intensive Care	12		

General surgery beds were subsequently reduced to 32 and cardio-thoracic beds increased to 54, with the 32 displaced surgery beds moved to a ward in the old Baguley Hospital.

In the July 1954 issue of the Baguley Sanatorium magazine, *San Toy,* the following information was given about Dr Thomas Wilson who succeeded Dr Trayer as Medical Superintendent, a position he held during the formative years of the new hospital.

SAN TOY welcomes Dr Thomas M Wilson who is succeeding Dr Trayer as physician superintendent of Baguley. And to nail the inevitable, fact-less gossip circulating round the parish pump "Notebook" presents the facts by - Dr Wilson himself.

Born in Dumfies, Scotland, in 1919 Dr Wilson his claim to fame on his birth day. For he was the first child to be born in the parish manse, where his father, now dead, was a Minister of the Church of Scotland. Educated at Dumfries Academy which claims Sir James Barrie, author of the immortal Peter Pan, as a pupil - Dr Wilson began his medical studies at Edinburgh University in 1937, graduating MB, Ch.B in 1942. That year he was appointed House Physician at the Royal Infirmary, Edinburgh, and also began his military service, three years of which he spent as Medical Officer to an infantry battalion in the Parachute Regiment.

Strangely reticent about his military career, Dr Wilson left the army in 1946, with a lot of experience which no amount of civilian practice could provide, and a Military Cross about which he refuses to say anything. From 1946 to January 1949, (he became a Member of the Royal College of Physicians in 1947), he held post-graduate appointments in Edinburgh Royal Infirmary. From January until November of 1949 he was Medical Registrar at the Royal Victoria Hospital, Edinburgh. Then, like all true Scots, he came south of the border to become House Physician at Brompton Hospital, London. From March 1950 to July 1953 he was Resident Medical Officer at Brompton, becoming Medical Registrar there in August 1953.

He claims considerable enthusiasm "but little prowess" at swimming, football and rugby, likes fishing and gardening, but delights in interfering with mechanical devices, usually, he says, "with disastrous results".

So there it is. Most of the "low-down" on Dr Wilson, and on behalf of all San Toy readers, "Notebook" welcomes him, his wife, and their children to a long, happy and successful stay at Baguley Sanatorium.

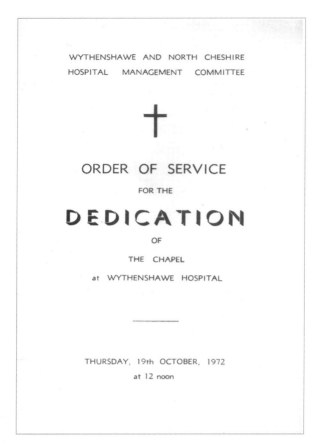

WYTHENSHAWE AND NORTH CHESHIRE
HOSPITAL MANAGEMENT COMMITTEE

✝

ORDER OF SERVICE

FOR THE

DEDICATION

OF

THE CHAPEL

at WYTHENSHAWE HOSPITAL

———

THURSDAY, 19th OCTOBER, 1972
at 12 noon

*Order of Service at the Dedication of the Chapel at Wythenshawe Hospital
following relocation of the Chapel from the Recreation Hall to new premises*

Included in the dedication was a memorial plaque to Dr TM Wilson.

In the 1970s and 1980s, Wythenshawe Hospital became one of the busiest hospitals in the North West. It emerged as the major accident centre for the area and was tested in this role with the 22nd August 1985 Manchester Airport crash. The hospital's emergency plans rolled into action and all departments demonstrated their ability to respond to a major incident.

It was in this period that the work load increased considerably and all departments appointed extra staff. Some of the new consultants were Mr Brian Hancock, General Surgery; Dr I Manns, Dr P Jones Dr J Crampton, General Medicine; Dr E Varley, Dr T Ormston, Dr E Thompson, Dr M Tobias, Dr P Challen, Dr P Hall, Anaesthesia; Dr A Horrocks, Dr M Aird, Dr I Turley, Dr A

Mattison and Dr Beton, Radiology; Dr J Wynn and Dr M Fouracres, Obstetrics and Gynaecology; Mr P Jones in Ear, Nose and Throat joined Mr W Nasser.

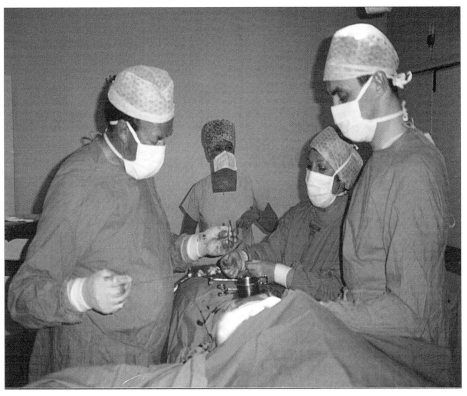

Author with surgical team

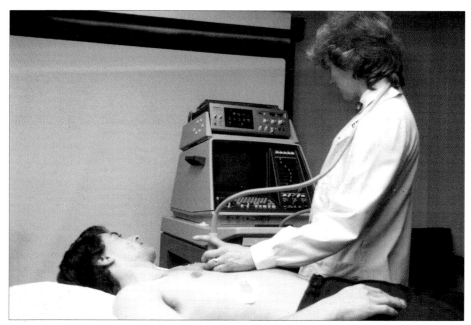

Echo Cardiograph machine donated by the British Heart Foundation 1985

Baguley wards, Recreation Hall, and Wythenshawe wards

Hutted area after demolition and prior to building of Acute Unit

Ward F3

Heart Transplant Unit

OPTION 1

OPTION 2

Proposed plan of the tram links to Wythenshawe Hospital

Present-day Wythenshawe Hospital

In 1994, the bulldozers finally moved in to demolish the A Wards - 40 years after they were supposed to come down. It was the end of an era but marked the start of a multi-million pound expansion programme of hospital facilities.

The 12 wards had been built during the war as temporary accommodation but continued in use as medical and chest wards and the speech therapy department until 1993. These facilities were then relocated to the North West Lung Centre and other parts of the hospital.

Up to 1994, South Manchester Health Authority (SMHA) was responsible for running Withington and Wythenshawe Hospitals as well as Christie Hospital. There was duplication of facilities across the three sites and the maintenance of the ageing fabric of the Withington buildings was a constant drain on resources. In 1989-90, the SMHA revenue costs were £111.5 million, of which £94.6 million was spent across the three hospitals. In the early 1990s, the decision was taken to rationalise Withington and Wythenshawe Hospitals.

Demolished wards - old EMS huts

129

As part of major reforms of the NHS, hospitals became self governing trusts. The SMHA was split into three Trusts: Christie Hospital NHS Trust, South Manchester University Hospitals NHS Trust (SMUHT) and Mancunian Community Health NHS Trust.

SMUHT, which included Withington and Wythenshawe Hospitals, developed a rationalisation strategy based on Wythenshawe as the main 'state-of-the-art' in-patient hospital and Withington as the community hospital with out-patient facilities and a few special units. These proposals caused considerable local opposition and a 'Save Withington Hospital' campaign led to years of public consultation.

During this period the Trust did not stand still, carrying on with investment in buildings and patient services at Wythenshawe Hospital and, to some extent, moving towards the goal of making it the main focal point for in-patient care. A new day case service was established at Withington Hospital. In 1995, SMUHT had an annual income of £150 million and a staff of 5,500 to deal with more than 75,000 in-patients and day cases, 300,000 out-patients and 90,000 attendances at the Accident and Emergency Departments. To rationalise such a huge organisation was a mammoth task.

Since the formation of the Trust in 1994, the main highlights have been:

1. The North West Lung Centre received a £1 million grant from Glaxo to build a research unit.

2. Two new state-of-the-art cardiac catheterisation laboratories opened at a cost of £1.6 million.

3. A purpose-built £1.25 million cystic fibrosis unit was opened to take the service transferred from Monsall Hospital. This was made possible by a large donation from the Bradbury Trust.

4. The Baguley Suite opened for day cases needing local anaesthetics and ophthalmic services.

5. A £2.8 million new maternity unit opened following the move of Withington maternity services to Wythenshawe.

The new Wythenshawe Acute Unit, financed and built under the Government's Private Finance Initiative, was officially opened in May 2002 and marked the completion of the first phase of a major development on the Wythenshawe Hospital Site. The £113 million investment included £66 million from the Private Finance Initiative (PFI) and £47 million in Treasury funding.

The following press release was issued by the Trust at the opening:

Wythenshawe Hospital provides a wide range of general health services to local people and specialist services to a wider population. It is the centre for all emergency, critical and acute in-patient care in South Manchester. Its fields of specialist expertise lie in the treatment of heart and lung conditions, including specialist surgery and transplantation, the treatment of burns, plastic surgery and cancer.

Facilities in the 319-bedded Acute Unit include:

*   *A state-of-the-art Accident and Emergency department with a dedicated resuscitation suite and a separate mini A & E for children with an external courtyard play area.*

*   *A 12 bed burns centre.*

The new Wythenshawe Acute Unit

Aerial view of Wythenshawe Hospital - 2002

*   A 10 bed coronary care unit.

*   A 17 bed intensive care/high dependency unit.

*   6 operating theatres.

*   5 medical and 5 surgical wards.

*   X-ray department.

*   Fracture clinic.

*   Renal unit.

*   Well researched design - all specialist areas such as the state of the art
    accident and emergency department, the critical care areas, the wards and
    operating theatres have been designed with input from clinical staff to
    ensure they meet the needs of each individual service.

*   *Tastefully decorated patient accommodation in either four-bedded ward bays or in single rooms with en-suite facilities. Each bed has its own satellite TV, radio and telephone system.*

*   *Comfortable, pleasant and therapeutic surroundings with landscaped gardens and internal courtyards, specially designed to promote well being and recovery.*

A new 77-bed Mental Health Unit, which was also part of the Private Finance Initiative, opened at the same time and is now part of Manchester Mental Health and Social Care Trust. The second phase of the development includes a 44-bed Rehabilitation Unit, a state-of-the-art Day Treatment Unit and additional out-patient facilities.

The Treasury also funded a £2 million extension to the Children's Unit which opened in October 2000 and a new £7 million Education and Research Centre which opened in November 2001.

The new Millennium has ushered in yet another phase in the history of the Baguley site - with a building programme that is equipping Wythenshawe Hospital to be the focus of acute care in South Manchester, while its sister hospital at Withington takes on a new lease of life in primary care. Wythenshawe Hospital is set to continue providing health care in the tradition of community service that was established a century ago when Baguley Sanatorium first opened its doors.

Appendices

Memories

Memories provided by John Dark - Chest and Heart Surgeon, Baguley and Wythenshawe Hospitals

Baguley Sanatorium

In 1949, when Mr Dark was appointed to the post of Medical Officer to the Surgical side, the Sanatorium was full of patients, some of whom had been there for years. Tuberculosis was an awful disease, most of the patients were young, in their late teens or twenties. There were many ex-servicemen, especially from the Navy. The treatment was bed rest (for months or years), fresh air and good food. The cubicles, 6A and B, 8A and B, upstairs and downstairs, were open at either end on to open corridors. The doors were like stable doors with upper and lower parts opening separately. If the weather was bad the lower part of the door was closed and sometimes red rubber sheets were put over the bed clothes to keep them dry. It was clear that any success engendered by the treatment must have been based on the tenet that if the patient could survive the treatment he could survive the disease.

Mr J Dark
Consultant Cardio Thoracic Surgeon

The other treatments were artificial pneumothorax, (phrenic crush and pneumoperitoneum) and major surgery - either staged thoracoplasty, lobectomy or pneumonectomy,

Artificial pneumothorax was discussed as a theoretical treatment to rest the lungs to promote recovery in 1882 by Italian physician, Carlo Fornanini, but he did not make a clinical trial until 1888. Meanwhile, JW Hulke, a surgeon, and W Cayley, a physician, both of the Middlesex Hospital, had inserted a double rubber catheter into one side of the chest of a twenty-one-year old man who had been admitted to the hospital after suffering a very large haemorrhage (haemoptysis) from the lung. The operation took place on 10 March 1885, but the patient died five days later from the effects of another haemoptysis.

Between 1888 and 1911, Fornanini carried out eighty-six of these operations: he found that air was absorbed too quickly and started to use nitrogen instead. In Britain, interest was aroused by Parry Morgan and Leonard Colebrook of St Mary's, where the first successful injection of nitrogen was carried out on 11 August 1910. But only four hundred cases could be traced in the world literature in 1910; this is a minute number when related to the terrible prevalence of tuberculosis.

Another method of resting the lung was destruction of the nerve supply of the diaphragm, the large respiratory muscle separating the chest cavity from the abdomen. In 1913, PL Friedrich suggested that the nerve should not be cut but crushed; the temporary damage would allow a period of rest, but the nerve would be capable of recovering and of taking up its function again. The 'phrenic crush' was often used as a preliminary to more extensive operations upon the chest.

Original Baguely operating theatre block

There was one other quite commonly performed procedure, the Jacobeas operation. This was the division of adhesions preventing the proper collapse of the affected lung in the case of a AP. It was done by using a cautery and a thoracoscopic telescope. These battery powered instruments were manipulated, having been inserted through a canulae that had been pushed into the pleural cavity. It is interesting to recall that this was very early 'keyhole surgery'.

Polythene pack Plombage was a bit of a disaster. The packs were made on the premises and consisted of polythene envelopes filled with polythene tape and sterilised in formalin vapour. In one or two instances, the formalin was too strong eventuating in widespread tissue destruction. One case was where the Brachial Plexus was agonisingly involved.

The surgery was carried out in the Baguley Theatre. It had originally been the night staff rest room. There were two theatres. The one at the left hand end was for major surgery. It had an extraordinary multi-tube overhead neon light which could not be focused at all and merely gave a strong benign diffuse illumination. The lighting was so bad that the surgeons were early users of flexible lights hooked into the chest cavity and also headlamps. In some cases a battery powered headlamp was used but it got so hot that it often burned the assistant's forehead or ear when leaning forward to help.

This scrub-up basin actually came from the main theatre and was used by the author. It now stands in his garden filled with flowers

There were two large porcelain scrub-up basins in the theatre. Ventilation was provided by opening one of the sash windows which, unfortunately let in the flies which usually enjoyed the more pungent charms of the adjacent piggery. There was an anaesthetic room next door. At the other end of the building was the other theatre which only had portable lights on stands and was only used for

138

minor surgery and endoscopies. Commonly both theatres were working together. There were three Recovery Rooms which must have been fairly unique early Intensive Care beds. There were necessary in view of the long distances from the wards. All patients were kept there overnight.

The hospital x-ray Department was also situated in the middle of the theatre block. In it were held the twice-weekly screening sessions required to check out the state of the Artificial Pneumothorax and Phrenic crush and Pheumoperitoneum.

Pathology Services

The hospital pathology laboratory was on the left hand side of the drive down from Baguley entrance, now demolished.

History of Pathological Services

1917 First record of laboratory work done by the dispensing assistant and consisted of examining sputa for TB bacillus.

1918 20% of patients were discharged service personnel.

1922 20 years after opening the hospital the average was 2 tests per patient. The beds were increased to 333.

1930's About 500 patients admitted each year.

City of Manchester Pathology Service set up for Crumpsall, Booth Hall, Withington, Prestwich and Baguley. Main laboratory at Crumpsall and subsidiary rooms at Withington and Booth Hall but only one staff which consisted of 1 pathologist and 1 assistant pathologist, 5 technicians, 2 laboratory boys and 1 cleaner. The pathologist was Dr G D Dawson and assistant pathologist was Dr George Stewart Smith but in 1938 Dr Dawson became ill and had to retire and Dr Stewart Smith was appointed City Pathologist.

Cardiac Surgery

Thoracic surgery at that time was a very new speciality. Effectively it had had to await the event of the endotracheal tube and positive pressure ventilator before real intrathoracic surgery could take place.

When Mr Dark got to Baguley, curare - a refined South American arrow poison - had arrived. They could paralyse the patient with curare which meant that ordinary chaps could get an endotracheal tube in the right orifice, most of the time, and they could do the respiring of the patient just by rhythmically squeezing a rubber bladder fitted with appropriate valves, and they could do without the dreaded Cycloproprane and keep the patient only lightly anaesthetised (sometimes too lightly) by using relatively safe Nitrus oxide. In those days anaesthetists worked very hard having to keep squeezing that bag continuously for hours at a time. It was not long, however, before those cunning chaps had machines, at first very noisy ones, but they soon progressed towards the more sophisticated equipment which, apart from doing the job quietly and efficiently, had room on top for a coffee cup and the Manchester Guardian.

Baguley Sanatorium was full of patients with pulmonary tuberculosis. It is difficult to appreciate nowadays what a scourge it was 50 years ago. Tuberculosis was a prolonged, debilitating and often fatal disease.

The standard operation was thoracoplasty. It was carried out in 2 or even 3 stages at fortnightly intervals so as to give time for stiffening of the chest wall, at the site of the previous stage. Looking back on it, this was an enormous ordeal for these young people. Most of them were in their early 30's or 20's and they were already debilitated by their disease and what then passed for treatment, namely long-term bed rest and exposure in open air wards to the prevailing elements.

There was a Chief Assistant called James Glennie, a forthright Aberdonian. Mr Dark and James Glennie had the 2 operating theatres at Baguley to themselves for most of the week. James Glennie told Mr Dark that he would help him with 100 endoscopies, 1 lobectormy, 1 pheumonectomy, 1 thoracoplasty and then he would be on his own.

During the phase of overdue expansion Mr Dark was lucky to be appointed first Senior Registrar and then Consultant at the unseemly age of 31 in October 1952. At the same time another young man called Gordon Jack, was also appointed.

Rather than build a custom designed unit at the Baguley Hospital, in 1950 the

Board moved the non-TB part of the unit to Park Hospital, Davyhulme and they did not get it altogether again at the new Wythenshawe Hospital until 25 years later.

The antituberculous drugs, Streptomycin and Para-Amino-Salicylic, which appeared in the early 1950s allowed more extensive surgery to be employed, and then in 1957, when used for the first time for long periods rather than in 6 week courses, they made surgery obsolete. The waiting lists suddenly disappeared. By 1957 they were 14 months long and they absolutely disappeared overnight.

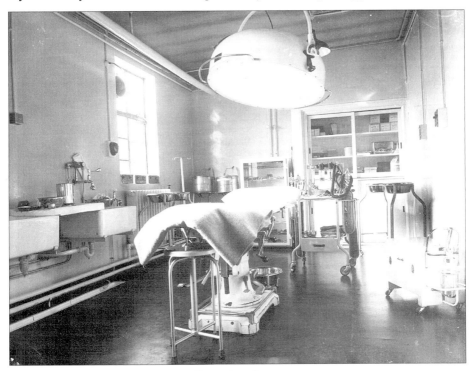

Operating theatre

Heart Surgery

It is doubtful if ever in history one group of surgeons had enjoyed such exciting and demanding challenges in their day to day professional lives as was enjoyed in Manchester.

Before 1969 there were no Cardiologists at Wythenshawe. Dr Geoffrey Wade was relied upon for his unstinting generosity who, when requested, would see patients at 7.30 a.m. on the Thursday morning.

The Board were asked repeatedly for a Cardiologist and eventually Gordon Jack and Mr Dark were invited to go before the Medical Advisory Committee and make their case. Every Thoracic Surgical Unit in the Country had been written to by Mr Dark and had ascertained that, in fact, ours was the only Unit in the UK without a Cardiologist and a Department of Cardiology. This fact shamed them into it and Dr Colin Bray was appointed and given a Kencast hut to work in. He and his three colleagues have built the Department up and it is now reliably quoted, by figures from the Cardiac Society, as the unit with the biggest throughput of patients in the UK.

There was a very amusing episode associated with a mechanical pump because financial assistance was applied for to the Regional Board and they did in fact grant £25.00, this fact was recorded in the minutes of the meeting of the Board and was picked up by a smart reporter. The next day the Daily Mail had a leading article which said that "Manchester Surgeons Invent plastic heart" and the medical correspondent of the Manchester Guardian, may he be forgiven, said that this apparatus was a great advance on anything yet designed as it was able to work for adults as well as children. What was not know was that Professor Ian Aird at the Postgraduate Medical School, at Hammersmith, had been given £25,000 to produce a heart lung machine and his sponsor's got on to him and said "how is it they can do it in Manchester for £25.00?" you haven't yet done it at the Hammersmith for £25,000. A deputation had to be sent to London to mollify him.

The first full bypass, however, using commercial apparatus was carried out at the Baguley hospital in 1960. The condition was an atrial septal defect and, in fact, the operation was carried out by Mr Athol Riddell, who was then the Senior Lecturer at the Royal Infirmary. The Author later worked with Mr Athol Riddell in Bristol for 2 years. His help and experience was greatly valued in the laboratory.

Open heart surgery was started in the old Baguley Theatres doing one open heart operation every fortnight, but in 1965 Mr Dark made his first visit to the USA, to Houston, Texas, where to his undying astonishment he saw Denton Cooley doing three open hearts and five major vascular operations every day, and he came back determined to drive everyone to these heights. It was not easy but at

Wythenshawe they reached the numbers accomplished in Houston in 1965, just short of a 1,000 patients per year.

Since 1980 improvements in anti-rejection treatment and, in particular, Cyclosporin A, have made heart transplantation respectable and in fact very successful. Manchester has been lucky. When the Department of Health indicated that, because of the success of this sort of surgery, (about 75% of patients are expected to live for 5 years), that they would designate a fourth centre, the local Health Authority had the foresight to give their permission to start doing this work on the proviso that it was supported entirely from charitable monies. The business of raising cash for this purpose took up rather a lot of time. From September 1986 to 2002 over £6 million was raised. The hospital was designated as the fourth UK heart transplant centre in December 1987 thus reaching the first aim. The first heart transplant was carried out at Wythenshawe in April 1987 and between that date and October 1989 a total of 56 operations with 45 survivors were carried out.

Newall House

Nearly all the nurses were resident in Newall House across the road. The Christmas Dinner Dance was held there and was a big event. It was allegedly tee-total but, Dr Trayer, the Medical Superintendent, had a little room with booze in it for everyone except the Matron.

The doctors had a big dining room in the main Baguley block. Excellent food was served by two uniformed maids, it was of course all free.

There was absolutely no parking problems. Mr Dark, who lived 17 miles away at Oldham, travelled each day comfortably in 25 minutes.

There were staff tennis courts behind the Newall House side and there was a splendid crown bowling green where the new Maternity Hospital was and, as it

Nurses Home Canteen - 1951

Hospital tennis courts

Staff Dining Room - 1951

was in front of 8A and B, we could bowl there whilst being on call.

In 1949 the senior medical staff consisted of Dr Trayer and his deputy, a Glaswegian called Dr Cuthbert. The residents were nearly all Irish - Kevin Murphy and Malachy O'Connor and Leslie Doyle. There were also two visiting Chinese doctors who were quite delighted that the Communists under Mao had just overrun their country.

The EMS Hospital was really quite smart. There were sixteen wards, a theatre and x-ray department, a laboratory, a residency and a dining room. The wards had central coke stoves.

Our wards were   14 -   non-tuberculous men.

                                     16 -   half women and half children (almost all of whom had bronchiectasis).

The junior medical staff was a mixed bunch. The resident in Plastic surgery was a Northern Ireland chap called Mr Dickie. He was quite senior, very wise and greatly respected. He had spent most of the war in China and we could never

Emergency Medical Services huts - Wards 14 and 16

find out what he did there. It was suspected that he had been some kind of Missionary. Moira Cole looked after the Christie patients. She too was from Northern Ireland with a very soft voice. She finished up as a Consultant at the Christie hospital. Desmond Pengelly was there and another remarkable man, Malcolm Towers, who was a sort of electronic genius. He made his own ECG machine. He was very brainy indeed, his function was to look after the soldiery. He later became involved in Cardiology at Harefield. The last one was David Linders who was attached to the non-tuberculous surgical side, but he wasn't interested in surgery and looked after the medical aspects.

The patients from the EMS side were taken to the theatre in Baguley on a trolley which was wheeled along the path between the huts. If it was raining the patient was covered over by red rubber sheets. After an overnight stay the patient was then brought back the same way.

The x-ray department was fairly primitive. About four or five Bronchograms were made on children every Saturday morning. The method was simple. The child was rendered unconscious with Chloroform and Ether bronchoscoped. The deep breathing was induced by administering CO_2. The mouth was opened and 20 mls of Lipiodol was poured in. Of course it was all inhaled. The child

X-ray Department - 1960

147

was positioned by various postures of one's own invention and the x-rays were taken. The results were excellent. It was a very quick method and there was never any crisis or life-threatening situation.

It was a happy place, the administration was minimal, the Superintendent was in charge. He had a clerk to help him and there was a lady who looked after the accounts. There was also a marvellous man called Mr Hall. He was getting near retirement but was very fit. He had a loud voice and people tended to do what he said. He was the Steward and his duties were many but, the chief one was that of being in charge of stores and the ordering of everything to make the hospital tick, from food and blankets to medicines and instruments. In his spare time he ran a very successful pig farm kept going on all the hospital slops. The money went into the hospital coffers. He was regarded with great affection. Shortly after he retired he was sadly knocked off his bike on the Chester road and killed.

Memories in a letter from Sheila Monether - Nursing Staff

Nursing in Manchester in 1940s

I awoke to the sound of the alarm clock and the clanking of the trams on their way to and from the city along Oxford Road. There was something different about this day, gradually the facts came into my mind, "They" were coming. Looking through the window at the grey morning mist, the half-lights of the buses, trams and streetlights made pools of fuzzy light on the wet road and pavement.

The ward was ready for today's admissions, military, medical or surgical? No information was given, but probably both. Arriving in the afternoon or evening. We got used to not knowing what, where or when. There was permanent blackout on the wards; the windows bricked up on the outside to the top, as it was on all the ground level wards.

We were to go with the ambulances to the station to meet the hospital train. We had received military admissions before but this one was different, they were German prisoners of war, taken in a French hospital and evacuated to make room for allied casualties. We all had sweethearts, brothers and friends on active service and this had needed some thought. But really a patient was a patient and the POW's would have to be cared for as we hoped our boys would be if in similar circumstances. There was no other way we could cope with it.

The ambulances were lined up, backs to the platform where the train was expected. There were small stumps of rusting iron where the railings had been. All railings and gates had been removed early in the war to be melted down together with old and surplus pots and pans towards the making of armaments. As we waited on the platform we went over the procedure for loading the ambulances. The medical orderlies on the train would bring off the worst cases first and as each ambulance was full it would leave for the hospital. Looking out over the city were the same fuzzy lights, the blackened half-holes of destruction from the air, in the grey mass, which was Manchester in the 1940's. There was an air of waiting, waiting for the next air raid, waiting for the end of this terrible war... waiting for a train. The rain was drizzling down, raining the tears of so many heartbreaking partings on this long, now empty platform.

"Can you speak German?" I whispered to the nurse standing next to me. "Only what I learnt at school and I don't think that will be much use here", she said. "Same as me, I can remember some phrases which could come in handy like "do you understand" and "what is the matter?" but I doubt if I will be able to understand their answer", I said. I believe matron speaks fluent German", she said. "Oh great! I can't see her being on hand every time a patient needs to tell us all the intimate details of his inner workings!"

"I wish we'd had more time to prepare", my friend sighed. "C'est la guerre". "That's French" - Our laughter seemed to ring out horribly loud, and we got the inevitable look of disapproval from a group of officers standing nearby. But we needed to laugh and were saved from reprimand by the arrival of the train.

I was told to go with the first ambulance and when I saw the first patient off the train I wondered if I would even get him to the hospital alive. Both legs amputated and abdominal wounds. I am pleased to say that he was eventually repatriated. There were six patients to each ambulance and it seemed to take so long before we had our full load and were on our way to the hospital.

A team of doctors made their first round of the patients with the help of one of the patients, a German Officer who spoke English, translating. It took hours. Another staff nurse and I followed the doctors, renewing the dressings, the first dressings for over three days, they were in a dreadful state. In the days after this it took the two of us, working only on dressings, two days to get round the ward, then start over again. There was no Penicillin in those days , we did have Sulphonamides which we thought were marvellous, but before that infection took a long time to clear up and needed very careful nursing.

We need not have worried about our attitude to the Germans. It was immediately apparent, even allowing for the exhaustion of three days travel, that they were in a very bad way. Many had amputations operated on in emergency conditions and performed by the guillotine method. The German Officer who spoke English, worked tirelessly, although wounded himself, to help the doctors translating and reassuring the patients. With his help the tense atmosphere in the ward improved in a matter of days and, although never friendly, they eventually managed to laugh at our schoolgirl German and usually pretended not to understand a word of it.

The British Army provided us with a twenty four hour guard on the ward, although of necessity, I suppose, they were men who were not considered to be of use on active service and, quite frankly, I don't think they would have been much use to us either. Fortunately we did not have any discipline problems. They had to wear sneakers to maintain a certain amount of quiet, but that didn't do anything to improve their slovenly appearance. They seemed to spend all their time drinking tea and chatting up the nurses.

We moved departments every three months so I was not there when the Germans were eventually repatriated, but I know that out of the forty on the ward I worked on, only one died.

I moved to another hospital and the patients there were British service men on long-term treatment, especially skin grafting. The men burned in their tanks faced years of returning to hospital for the gradual - oh so gradual - building up of shattered faces and limbs, the making of fingers so that a hand could grip again.

No language difficulty here except when some of them returned to the ward from the local pub. They went to their pieces of rubber tubing, the only way they could drink through the one hole left for the purpose in the wired-up shattered jaw. After a few drinks their language was very colourful, then it was my turn to pretend I didn't understand what they said.

The high spirits hiding the pain and disillusionment, were hard to take at times, as were the ghastly nightmares - leaping from their beds in the night, eyes wild and shaking with fear. Reliving the event, which was their last on active service.

We had two specialist surgeons, one an Australian who did all the "big" work, flaps to build up tissue etc. And a Spaniard who did all the fine, delicate work, mostly on faces. He was an artist using photographs and sketching the improvements he was aiming at.

The Germans were our enemies but somehow they were also individual people with homes and families, drawn into a war situation as we were.

I wonder how I would have felt if I had known then about the atrocities of the war camps and refugee camps. The Japanese were something else, I really felt a hatred and fear of them, convinced I would always feel that way. However, years after the war I was returning to England from the U.S.A. and found myself seated on the plane next to two Japanese men. They didn't speak much English but we carried on some sort of conversation, even laughing and joking. Sometime later it occurred to me that they were JAPS and I had TALKED TO THEM!

For many the world came to an end in wartime, for the rest of us, life goes on.

Memories in a letter from Malcolm Towers - 29 June 2001

My National Service covered 1947-49. The last 18 months or so were spent at Baguley where I was a junior officer looking after soldiers with pulmonary tuberculosis. Our patients were diagnosed during their military service and sent to us to await a vacancy in a civilian sanatorium near their home. Some of them were with us for a year or more. The drugs were just coming in towards the end of my time. People nowadays have no idea what a dreadful thing tuberculosis was. It was fairly ordinary to put up a film of a young man with large cavities at both apices and say "he will be dead in 18 months". He would be and nothing much could be done about it. Treatment was rest and collapse of the affected lung or lungs by artificial Pneumothorax (AP), Thoracoplasty or Plombage (occasionally), or Phrenic crush and Pheumoperitoneum (PP). If I remember correctly we had 4 wards in the hutted EMS hospital and a ward for administration. We had no female patients. When I arrived the unit was run by Major Nagley, who operated a very liberal (most thought too liberal) regime. Patients who did not have "open" tuberculosis, i.e., were not coughing up

151

tubercle bacilli, were allowed generous weekend leave. We had comparatively few patients on absolute bed rest. When Major Nagley left, I would guess in the early part of 1949, he was not replaced and Dr Trayer took over the running of the unit. A much more restrictive and conventional regime was imposed. We (the RAMC doctors) dealt with the induction and maintenance of AP's and PP's, but surgical procedures were carried out by Mr Graham Bryce and his team. Mr Coello - "the Spanish surgeon" - cut a rather glamourous figure and many of our patients would ask that he should do their thorcoplasties. Mr Coello had artistic talents and drew the most beautiful illustrations of his adhesion divisions as well as cartoons (see below).

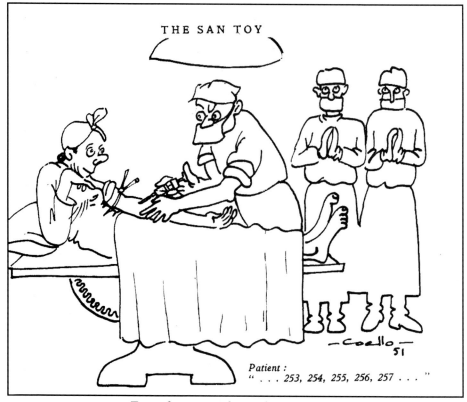

Typical cartoon drawn by Mr Coello

Major Nagley was in charge of the RAMC team when I arrived and Dr Kevin Murphy (a lady doctor) was his deputy. There was another Kevin Murphy - a man - on the sanatorium staff. Later Dr Lindars and Dr Shapiro arrived. They both lived locally so they stayed at home, though in the RAMC. Desmond Pengelly arrived towards the end of my time.

Beside our 4 wards in the EMS hospital there were an additional 6 - 8 wards. The X-ray department (Mrs Lomas) and the dental department (David Llyon) occupied one and the plastic unit at least another two. Mr McDowell's' favourite operation was to use the skin of the abdominal wall - hence "hand in tum". I was called by his ward sister one day because a patient was not coming round after his anaesthetic. I asked what I should do and she rang the theatre. We were instructed to give 5 cc of Coramine IV - which I did. The patient sat up and coughed.

I lived in the main part of the hospital and ate with the rest of the staff. We were looked after very well in those days of rationing. Amongst the junior staff the great characters were Vincent England Sherburn and Kevin Murphy (the male doctor). We had several Irish doctors.

Military service was a time of professional frustration. Doctors are used to days of 12 - 14 hours but we could finish our day in 2 - 3 hours. I became very fat and lazy. Much of my leisure was spent building bigger and better cathode ray oscillographs to display ECG's. One of the sanatorium patients, Teddy Gale, had a little room off the recreation area where he repaired radios. He generously allowed me to play there.

Baguley must have undergone the same sort of metamorphosis as Harefield. In the sanatorium world anything which could be done to-day could be done to-morrow, and was perhaps better done to-morrow. In the world of cardiology it were better done yesterday. When I arrived at Harefield in the 1960's I used to write "Action this day" on the X-ray forms because otherwise it could take a week.

For all its frustrations, I have happy memories of life at Baguley and the people there. I have kept in touch a little through Colin Bray (London Hospital trained as I was) and I see quite a lot of Richard Croxson.

The Sanatorium Staff consisted of:

Dr Trayer - Medical Superintendent
Dr James Cuthbert - Deputy Medical Superintendent

Dr Lewis Parker
Dr Vincent E Sherburn - "Sherbie"
Dr Kevin Murphy - "the Murphy of Kilrane" - "the Irish boy tenor"
Dr Donal Buckley

The Thoracic Surgery Staff consisted of:

Mr Graham Bryce - Thoracic surgeon
Mr JR Glennie - Snr., Registrar Thoracic Surgery
Mr John Dark - I don't remember very well - perhaps he did not eat in the mess.
Mr Coello

The Plastic Surgical Staff consisted of:

Mr Duncan McDowell - 'hand in tum'
Mr WR Dickie - Snr. Registrar Plastic Surgery

The Dental, Radiology Superintendent and Physiotherapist were David Lyon, Mrs Lomas and Miss Keltie respectively.

The RAMC personnel were:

Major Martin M Nagley
Lady doctor - Capt Kevin Murphy
DC Lindars
Mr Shapiro
Dr Desmond Pengelly
Malcolm Towers

Memories in a letter from Muriel D Bailey of Manchester - 16 August 1994

During the late 1920's an aunt and uncle were both patients and died of T.B. in Baguley Sanatorium. They died within a fortnight of each other leaving 2 little boys of 5 and 3. A relative wanted to take them but she was unable to get even a few shillings a week towards their keep from the Board of Guardians.

The children were taken to the workhouse. At that time, indeed, until the Second World War, children from the workhouse or homes left school at 14. Boys were sent on farms or as apprenticed into the Army. Girls were sent into service.

I had always been attached to the Girl Guides. It was decided by H.Q. that they would try to get a Guide Company started in the Sanatorium. It would have been about 1938. Older guides, of which I was one, were asked to visit the girls who were interested. The idea was to have a meeting once a quarter and in between to pass round a kind of scrap book containing one or two articles, a puzzle, quiz, jokes and a prayer to close. Actually it hardly got off the ground. It meant beds being wheeled from one ward to another and other girls could not walk far. All were ill. It was not unknown for a guide to be enrolled one week and dead a fortnight later.

It was a well known fact that if a patient was sent to Delamere Sanatorium then there was hope of recovery. If sent to Market Drayton, then about 50 percent

Block 7 - Female Ward for tuberculosis patients

and if to Baguley, then very little hope. I visited 29 guides over a 4 year period and only 1 survived and lived to be 65. Some went home to die or came back to die. The younger the girl, the sooner they passed on.

The Sanatorium was (during the war years) in the country surrounded by market

Block 6 - Male Ward for tuberculosis patients

gardens and fields of rhubarb and farms. On either side, inside the gates, were two long rows of cubicles, one for men and the other for women, and never the twain did meet! Some cubicles had 2 beds, some had 1 bed and a few had 4 beds. One door opened on to a long corridor and the other stood open at all times, even during the night I think.

There was a radiator at the foot of each bed, but I don't think it did much good. It was not unknown for snow to blow in and for rain to collect on the floor and to freeze. It was a spartan existence in the winter, scarves and gloves were the order of the day.

These were really sick people. I would visit a guide in one of these wards. Next time I visited I would go to the same ward; if I did not see her I never asked where she was, it upset the other patients.

The only remedy for T.B. was rest and fresh air. Then streptomicin was used, the old slums were knocked down or bombed and people had a better diet. And so the scourge of T.B. was beaten.

In 1954 as a ten year old, I moved to Baguley Sanatorium, my father, Dr Thomas Wilson, having been appointed as Consultant Physician Superintendent. As a family we lived in Baguley Lodge in the grounds on the corner of Floats Road and Clay Lane, (the house is now demolished). My father was in charge through the period that saw Baguley change to being a chest and heart hospital and through the merger with the old wartime Wythenshawe Hospital as new premises were built. He died in 1972 but my mother, Dr Olive Wilson, is alive and kicking.

My father took over from Dr Trayer and my mother will be able to tell you something of the battles he had in changing the regime. My mother is also in contact with many of the medical staff from the early years.

Dr Les Doyle, who was Deputy Superintendent in my father's time, is also still around. You will find that the new Wythenshawe Hospital has a Wilson ward and a Doyle ward, named after my father and Les.

As a boy with four younger brothers roaming the grounds I can tell you various tales. For example, unearthing the stock of World War One gas masks in the gardener's shed; earning illicit money be secretly buying cigarettes for the patients of Ward 7B who would signal to us from outside their horse boxes!

Information received from Barbara Moss relating to an article in the Manchester Evening Cronicle, 25 January 1941, about her Great Uncle, Alec Tinker.

Invalid's Song to de Gaulle

Fifty-eight year old Alec Tinker, who has been a patient in Baguley sanatorium for seven years, has written a song which he has dedicated to General de Gaulle.

He has sent a copy to the general and has received a reply thanking him 'for the spirit of co-operation which prompted your kind action'. Comrade Armies of Free Frenchmen, Comrade Armies of the Free. With the sons of Britain's Empire, In the air, on land, and sea. Fight to win your Country's freedom!

Let the Soul of France arise! March on, march on to victory, Bravo! Our French Allies.

The song is to be specially featured at a "General de Gaulle Dance" in aid of Free French War Charities at the Empress, Heaton Norris, on 31 January, when it is hoped that soldier vocalists will assist.

His famous song

Mr Tinker, who was the original singer of the famous song, "I do like to be beside the Seaside," and the pioneer of song writing for the motion picture, has sold about 200 songs since. At the age of 16 he sold his first song to a music hall artist.

"I wrote the present song because I am very much in sympathy with the Free French movement." Mr Tinker told the Evening Chronicle today

Alec Tinker
former editor of The San Toy Magazine

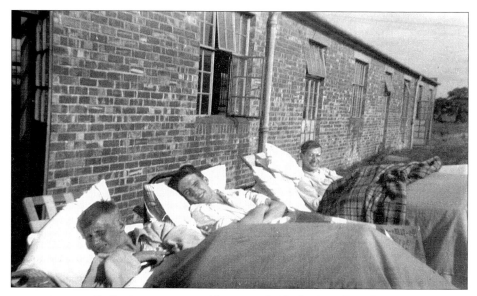

Patients were put outside to get the fresh air at Baguley

Memories in a letter from Jean Bright of Altrincham, Cheshire - 25 January 1994

I enclose photographs which may be of interest to you. (see previous page) When the weather was favourable beds were put outside as many patients were bedfast for quite a long time.

I started at Baguley in early 1946 until June 1948 and worked on Pavilion 11, the Burns and Plastic Surgery Unit all the time, both days and on nights. The two surgeons were Mr Champion and Mr Hamlyn and following Mr Champion, Mr McDowall. The Sisters at that time were Hayward, Sanders and Syers.

During my time on Pav II we had patients from all the services and in about 1947 we took civilians requiring plastic surgery because of burns and accidents. This Unit later moved to Withington.

Hospital work in those days was very different to now. We had 30/32 patients on the ward, sometimes having extra beds down the centre. There were two or three coke burning stoves in the centre. The smoke and dust from these was awful but I don't remember it ever causing cross infections on patients.

All bandages were washed and boiled on the ward, dried in the boiler room and re-rolled on a little wooden gadget. Dressings, etc., were prepared on the ward, packed into drums and taken to the Autoclave at the theatre.

Apart from normal nursing duties we cleaned the wards, moved the beds to the centre to polish the solid floors with a long handled "bumper" - a very strenuous job - no labour saving devices then, served meals, washed up when necessary and acted as general "dogs bodies". We never complained because there wasn't anyone to complain to. The hours were 8 a.m. to 8 p.m. with a couple of hours off during the day and two days off after 11 days. Nights were 8 p.m. to 8 a.m. I cannot remember what the pay was - I know it was very small - but we did the job because we wanted to, certainly not for the money.

Patients were able to obtain permission to go out for a short while and those that were able used to go across the bottom field, before the 'prefabs' were built, to go to the Royal Oak or elsewhere for a drink at night and, provided they brought a Guiness back for Sister Fisher, everything was alright. If anyone overstepped the mark they were before Major Samueld next day, he was in charge of Service Personnel.

Night Staff at Baguley Sanatorium - 1947
Front row - second left - Sister Fisher in charge of all wards
Back row - 1st left Nurse Dixon (known as Dixie) and Jean Bright

Prior to going to Baguley E.M.S. I worked as a Red Cross Nurse at a Military Convalescent Home in Lytham St. Annes, run by the Red Cross and St. John's until it was closed down.

Although my home was in Altrincham I lived in the Nurses Home at Baguley as transport was not so convenient in the 1940's. I became friendly with one of the Service patients on Pav II whose home was in Wallasey and we eventually married in 1949 (my name prior to marriage was Jean Horsfall) then became Roberts. Sadly he died in 1973 and I remarried in 1975 but alas I was once again widowed in 1983.

Memories in a letter from Mr I W Harrison of Wilmslow, Cheshire

My recollections are of a period just after the last war. I had joined the Army for National Service at Chester in June 1947 and completed my initial 4 weeks training at the Dale (Cheshire Regiment Depot). I had just received instructions

160

to report to Catterick when I was called into Chester Military Hospital. Apparently my Minirad had shown a shadow on my lungs.

I was detained in Chester from July to September 1947 when they finally decided I had T.B. I was then transferred to Baguley E.M.S. where I stayed until April 1948. We were confined to bed for the bulk of that time in a wooden hut, with doors that were kept open in all weathers. I had an A.P. *(Artificial Pneumothorax)* there, which had to be pumped up with air every week for the next 3 years. To assist in collapsing my lung they gave me a phrenic crush in the operating theatre of the civilian side of the hospital. I remember being wheeled quite a long way in the open air on a stretcher to the theatre. The occupational therapy was painting sputum pots!

In January 1992 I had a stroke and spent 5 days in Wythenshawe. The specialist, Mr Manns, who was accompanied by a group of students, seemed far more interested in me being a live ex-T.B. exhibit than in my stroke. He said my records would still be in the hospital and would examine them and show the students. My speech was very badly affected and I visited the Speech Therapist a number of times. I was amazed to find she was situated in the same group of huts that I was treated in during my 1947 stay. It wasn't the actual hut, but that was still standing; although I believe it has since been demolished.

Memories on a postcard from Miss J Blake

Yes! I was on the famous (or infamous) ward 7, Baguley San for 16 months. I was the girl who used to have a cork pop gun which made one hell of a bank to scare all the huge black Crows from the trees in front of our 'stables' (cubicles). Sister Hanlan was in charge of Ward 7 at the time. Doctor Sinton was there and a wonderful caring Polish doctor, Witold Zimborski.

Our cubicles were about six feet wide a door at each end. The top of the doors were always open and it was perishing cold, but they were left open throughout the year. When it rained or snowed we had a rubber sheet over the bottom half of our beds. I have so many stories - some of them absolutely hilarious; some of them tragic. And of course the sand bag treatment!

I had a nightly visitor perched on the bottom half of my door - a huge owl, which used to bring me presents - dead mice, worms etc. Stories too numerous to describe on a post card. Do you by any chance recall that wonderful lady, Pat

Simpson? An artist who brought joy into our lives.

Memories in a letter from Winifred Bromwich of Melton Mowbray - 13 February 1994

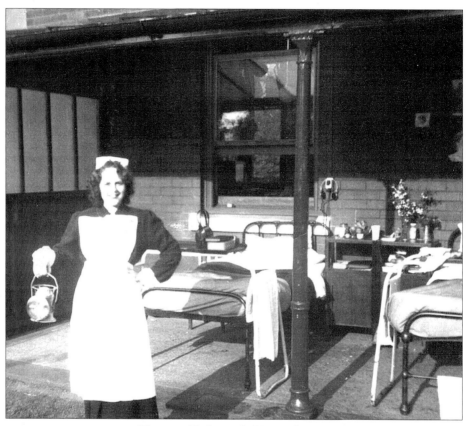

Florence Nightingale Hospital, Bury
where Winifred Bronwich was before going to Baguley

I was taken to Baguley Hospital in February 1954 and, on 22 February I had a left pneumoectomy. Mr Jack was the surgeon. He did not like us having visitors until five days after the operation, although some surgeons didn't' have any restrictions. I think it was to save us getting distressed while we were feeling low.

I was only a short time at Baguley before my 'op' so I cannot say a great deal about the place. I well remember being 'drummed' out of the ward - a ritual performed once one was on the trolley ready to go across for surgery. Tables and lockers were banged, in fact anything to make a continuous noise and give us a rousing send off! We used to hear the same ritual when the men in the ward next door went down. I don't know for how long it had been in practice but it was certainly memorable! Then it was outside to be wheeled along the paths to the operating theatre. We were kept overnight in the recovery room and wheeled back next morning to the ward.

I think it was about two weeks later when I was returned to the Florence Nightingale Hospital at Bury, where I had been a patient for the previous 10 months. The actual Sanatorium was out at Holcombe Brook. The Florence Nightingale Hospital was an isolation hospital, one block being taken over as overspill for the Sanatorium.

I am enclosing a photo of our veranda where I 'lived' for several months. It was taken when we had a fancy dress party and I am not one of the patients in the picture. The veranda I spent a short while on at Baguley seemed quite luxurious compared to ours. It had a low brick wall and large sliding windows built on. I don't know if they were ever closed. We had a rubber sheet put over our blankets if the weather was bad.

After six months recuperation I returned home to Didsbury. Two years later we moved to my husband's home to escape the 'smogs', since when I've kept remarkably well.

I know this is only a short account of Baguley, but perhaps another facet of its history.

Memories in a letter from Norma Millar, Timperley, Cheshire - 6 February 1994

All my life I have suffered from Bronchitis and have been a patient at Wythenshawe since 1948/9.

In 1948/9 I was sent to the then new Billet wards from M.R.I. where Mr Glennie and Mr Douglas were seeing patients for Sir Graham Bryce, (who I had seen from a small girl). I had my 15th birthday on Pav 16. Being January it was very cold and we used to huddle up round the combustion stoves, each ward had two placed in the centre of the ward, we fed them with coke or wood and I remember quite a lot of smoke.

Sincere Greetings

*Card received by
Norma Millar*

We could go out to the pictures, if not having treatment and would come back bearing fish and chips to share with friends who had not been able to go.

Sunday was treat day if over 14 years of age, you could have 20 cigarettes (I never smoked, but

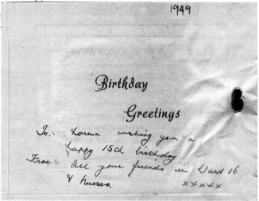

father was very glad of them).

17 was the skin graft ward for the badly injured forces of the war. Each branch of the service had wards further up the corridor, which in those days was just a concrete path linking the wards. Boy was it cold, if you were on the trolley going for a Broncogram or round to Baguley San operating theatre. In those days they did not put you to sleep, just froze the throat and got on with it. Not like today.

Mr Robinson had the E.N.T. clinic. He also had a clinic at St Anne's Hospital on Woodville Road, Altrincham. He operated on my nose and afterwards gave me a prescription

Copy of prescription

to get made up when ever I needed to. No payment then and could have repeats.

In 1959 I was very ill and went into the old Red Brick san wards for a month. Dr Doyle became my doctor and he was a wonderful man to me, I owe everything to his help, that I have just had my 60th birthday and led a near normal life, with care until now. Also Mr Wilson, a giant of a man, who would sit on the side of the bed with his arm round your shoulder and make everything come well again.

I was so thrilled when I knew they had named the new chest wards after these two great men.

1960 saw me back, it was a year exactly, in the wards opposite the main entrance on Floats Road. There upstairs on 1B I had our son, of course Dr Doyle came to see us before Gary was whisked off to Pendlebury hospital until I was discharged a month later. The maternity unit, as we know it now, was still on the drawing board.

The newspaper cutting relating to Radio Baguley was special to me because I knew Mary Glover, she went home to Knutsford but returned soon after and died.

Aerial View of Baguley Sanatorium
Photograph provided by Mrs F Walker of Stockport, Cheshire

Memories in a letter from Mrs E Evans, Audenshaw, Manchester - 16 August 1994

I went into Baguley Sanatorium in September 1938 and got my discharge 3 August 1940. I was still having treatment, so I used to go to Denmark Road for it. On 9 December 1942 the treatment stopped as my lung had healed. I used to go then every two months for checkups, after a while I stopped altogether.

You mention a military hospital but I don't remember one. When did it stop being a sanatorium? I often wonder about that. It used to be lovely round there, it was countryside, all fields. When you were getting better they let you out on walks, one walk was to Timperley village, which was very nice. They also could go home for a weekend. I remember one weekend 3 or 4 of us were going home. As we got out of the gate a car was coming past, the driver stopped, he said, "I suppose you are going on leave, can I give you a lift?" We had to walk to the end of the lane to get a bus to town. We all looked at each other because we knew that he thought we were nurses, so we didn't say we were not nurses, we

Patients at Baguley Sanatorium
The one playing the accordian is Mrs E Evans

166

just got in. I never forgot that man, if he had known we were patients he would never have stopped. I remember when I came out, I met a friend, she said, "I haven't seen you for a while." Like a fool I told her where I had been, her face was enough, she couldn't get away quickly enough. I never saw her again. So I thought, "Well I won't tell anybody again". Only my relatives know. They don't understand that you can get cured.

There was plenty of things to do in the hospital, there were whist drives, handycraft and putting, there was a chapel in the grounds, they would convert it to give concerts, there would be one at Christmas. The men could come to the ward at Christmas, there were records played, one came to me for a dance, he was a good dancer. I was enjoying myself when in came the nurse, she played hell with me. I was only on Bed 1, that means I could only get up once every day, I was in my dressing gown. Enclosed is a snap taken in the hospital, the one with the accordian is me. They seem to be able to cure T.B. very quickly now, it must be a new drug. In the hospital we had to rest a lot and fresh air and good food.

Memories in a letter from Mrs Joan McHully, Manchester - 23 January 1994

I have so many stories I could tell about friends I lost, the freezing cold conditions, the harsh conditions the doctors put us through, the months spent in bed without putting a foot on the floor, people who had spent 5 to 10 years in the sanatorium and were still not cured. I could relate the antics we got up to when we were allowed up. Sneaking out of the back gate. Sleeping on an open veranda to find, sometimes, a pig wandering in and many times waking to find a horse staring at you, they came from the farms at the back of the sanatorium. My mother used to sneak in the back way twice a week with big nourishing meals for me, going without herself as some food was still rationed. Not being able to talk to the male patients, but we always found a way round that. My friend and I got very friendly with two ex-soldiers (not from the military hospital at the back); when we were found the two lads were sent to Switzerland either to be cured or away from us. How we left friends in on a Friday when we were allowed home for weekends only to return Sunday to find that they had passed away. We did once go on the wards of the Military hospital when all the female patients who were getting better dressed up for a May Day procession, some of us going in very short skirts which brought a smile to a lot of the lads faces. There are so many tales I could tell, but it would be like a book.

When I went in the San I was under 6 stone, given three months to live at the most. Here I am 68 years old and 3 children and still working. People treated me like a leper when I was discharged, wouldn't have me in their houses, even refusing to work with me when I returned to Ferranti" in Moston.

I visited Wythenshawe Hospital some months ago to see a friend. My daughter and I wandered round the back where some of the San still stands, surprisingly. Our day room was still there, we used to have an old iron stove in there where we used to fry food as the fresh air gave us huge appetites. I wonder how many of the patients from my era are left.

I returned again to the new block of the San, which was a maternity wing in 1955. I was there 7 months having my first child, the doctors wanted to remove my left lung but I tossed a coin and decided to keep it.

Actually as my friends and I were getting better we had a smashing time in there, unknown to the doctors and staff.

Memories in a letter from Jean Hoyland, Cheadle, Cheshire - 7 February 1994

I worked at Baguley Sanatorium and Wythenshawe E.M.S., as they were called from 1951 to 1954, as a pathological technician. The laboratory served both hospitals at that time.

Baguley sanatorium was indeed solely concerned with the treatment of TB with referrals from Denmark Road Chest Clinic in Manchester. The treatment consisted mainly of fresh air but the patients who were able could walk in the grounds and there was a bowling green and tennis courts for patients and staff. We published our own magazine called the "San Toy" and there was a lot of occupational therapy available. Wythenshawe E.M.S. at that time was an amalgam of different wards, medical, surgical, radiotherapy (an overflow from Christie hospital), ENT and plastic surgery. The latter had developed from the need to treat burns injuries sustained during the war and remained the burns unit until it was transferred to Withington hospital.

I believe the reason for building the E.M.S. hospital was to treat injured from the forces. It was built like an army camp and conditions in these wooden huts were worse than any in the sanatorium, in winter the only form of heating was one stove in the middle of the ward.

The pathology laboratory at Baguley serviced both hospitals, part of South Manchester Hospital Management Group. We were responsible to Dr Stent who carried out the post mortems from the mortuary next to the pig farm and generally oversaw our work. She visited the lab twice a week.

Specimens for histology examinations were sent to Withington laboratory for analysis, as were biochemistry samples, but all haematology and bacteriology requests were performed at Baguley. Blood for transfusions was crossmatched for all surgery, a fair number of pneumonectomies were performed at Baguley. Sputums were analysed on all patients weekly, the number of Kochs bacillus present was used as a very crude prognosis until the availability of streptomycin. I can well remember the excitement when viewing the results of this drug on cultures. The staff of the path laboratory consisted of only one senior technician and two trainees, who were regularly called out to crossmatch blood.

Pathology Laboratory

I left in 1954 to pursue my interest in haematology and genetics at St. Mary's Hospital just as the plans for the new hospital were being developed. I still have happy memories of my colleagues of those days, Dr John Sinton was medical officer, Mr Champion, plastic surgeon, Mr Dark, chest surgeon and Mr Hall, Administration Officer, who lived in a house on Floats Road. I have recently been round the hospital and find that many of the old buildings still remain, although in disrepair for example, the pat. lab., dispensary and patients canteen.

Baguley Hospital Entrance

Memories in a letter from Michael Moores of Dukinfield, Cheshire - 24 January 1994

I was Medical Records officer at Baguley Hospital between 1960 and 1964. The hospital, which was quite separate from Wythenshawe Hospital, was in the process of changing from a TB sanatorium to a modern chest hospital. The main surgery was for carcinoma of the lung, but during that time, the first open heart operations were carried out, much to the joy of everyone.

There was a great atmosphere of hope at that time and it was a very good place to be. I had a staff of 9, 5 secretaries and 4 clerical staff, some of whom were at the chest clinic (out-patients) on Clay Lane.

The physician superintendent was the late Mr T M Wilson, a very great man. He had been decorated during the war and was a superb physician. I know from experience that he was able to keep some people alive from will power alone. His deputy was the likeable Dr L Doyle. There were also two doctors from the Manchester Chest clinic at Denmark Road who had beds there. The surgeons I remember were Mr J F Dark, Mr G D Jack, Mr H M Bassett, Mr Thompson and Mr Nicholson.

The hospital secretary was Mr R MacDonald, a most efficient man and a superb organiser.

Some of the wards were the old ones for TB cases. I do not think they had any heating and were like horse boxes, in that the top half of the doors opened.

Memories in a letter from Norah Leashon of Blackley, Manchester - 25 January 1994

My father died in 1924 of Tuberculosis. He spent some time at Baguley and I remember going with my mother in winter time to see him. He was in bed on an open veranda with other patients. Sometimes they had snow on the beds. He did not improve with the treatment there and eventually discharged himself as he preferred to come home to die, which of course he did in February 1924. I was about 10 years of age at the time and remember what a difficult journey it was to get to Baguley from Moss Side, Manchester, about 3 trams and a walk, especially trying in winter time. My mother was left with 4 children, the eldest being 16fi, to bring, no handouts from the state until the widow's pension came through eventually, fortunately my father had commenced paying National Insurance and was just within benefit date.

Memories in a letter from Reg Wray of Wythenshawe Road, Wythenshawe - 24 January 1994

I was interested to read your letter in 'POSTBAG' regarding Baguley Sanatorium. I and my two brothers were members of the SOUTH SALFORD SILVER BAND. We used to give our services to various causes and I remember the band going to Baguley Sanatorium. We used to give one concert in the afternoon and one in the evening. The nurses always looked after us very well and gave us a nice tea. We used to go to Hope Hospital, Salford as well.

I do not think there is another musical company that did more for charity than our local brass bands. A request from a church or hospital was never refused.

I would place the exact year at about 1932.

San Toy
The Baguley Sanatorium Magazine

This magazine was first published in August 1935 and apart from the war years continued until 1954. It included articles submitted by patients and played a major part in the morale of staff and patients.

The author has included a random selection of the material in the various issues.

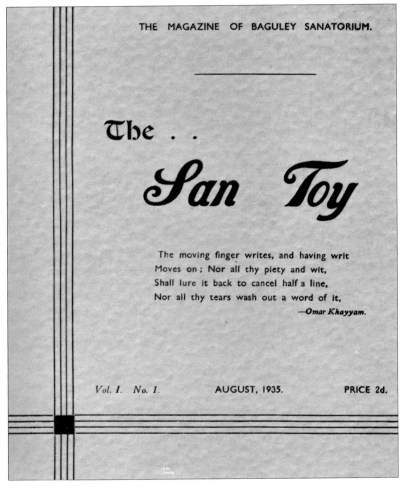

THE MAGAZINE OF BAGULEY SANATORIUM.

The . .

San Toy

The moving finger writes, and having writ
Moves on ; Nor all thy piety and wit,
Shall lure it back to cancel half a line,
Nor all thy tears wash out a word of it,
—*Omar Khayyam.*

Vol. I. No. 1.   AUGUST, 1935.   PRICE 2d.

Copy of the cover of the first San Toy August 1935

January 1946 Vol. VI No. 2

FOREWORD

To "The San Toy" by
The Lord Bishop of Manchester
The Right Rev Guy Warman, DD

I am very glad to hear that the Baguley Sanatorium has its Magazine once more, and that "San Toy," after six years of sleep has awakened again. If I may judge from its first new number, it has awakened in a very good temper. That is not always an easy thing to do. I hope it will continue to be cheery and bright, and help us all to be the same. I congratulate all concerned on the revival of your Magazine and wish it all success.

I am glad, for I know that the possession of a Magazine does help the spirit of goodwill and comradeship. It was the absence of that spirit that brought upon the world the tragedy of the war. The possession of it will bring us peace and prosperity and happiness. To that end we must all combine, and your magazine can help a little. But we can all do our share, and we all must. Every little helps though we do not always realise it. If we did, the world would be a better place, and nations at one end of the scale, and families and homes and people at the other would find greater happiness. We may not be great lights in the world, but even candles can do something, and mirrors reflect the sun, and we can do our bit.

May I send you every good wish for the blessing of God upon you in the coming year, and especially for greater health and greater happiness.

September 1948 Vol. VII No. 10

FAREWELL

At 11.0 a.m. on Friday, 2nd July a ceremony took place in the Recreation Hall to mark the passing over of the hospital from the Manchester Corporation to the South Manchester Hospital Management Committee. The Public Health Committee had the happy thought that the Chairman and Deputy Chairman of each hospital sub-committee, supported by various members of the committee, should visit their respective hospitals in order to take a formal farewell of the staff.

A truly representative gathering assembled in the Recreation Hall to receive the appreciative thanks of the Committee. Mrs Councillor Hill (the Chairman of the Hospital Committee), introduced Councillor Bowes (Deputy Chairman), who, in well chosen words, conveyed the Committee's appreciation of the loyal, harmonious working of the staff of this hospital over the years. He emphasised particularly that work in hospital was team work, and that every member of the team was essential to the efficiency and the achievement of the best results for the patients.

The Medical Superintendent (Dr H G Trayer) suitably replied, expressing the satisfaction that both Councillor Mrs Hill and Councillor Bowes were members of the South Manchester Committee and the fact that the former was the first chairman of this new committee. The Matron also replied, expressing thanks, and took the opportunity of stressing the need of recruitment to the depleted ranks of the nursing profession.

The Manchester Corporation Committee had made their last official visit to Baguley on Thursday 6th May.

October 1948

THE BEGINNING AND THE END

I spent two weeks in London during the war, and in that short time life began and ended for me. My first days in the city were lonely; the nights were full of danger for everyone, and few got any sleep. Towards the end of the first week I met a fellow I knew, and he invited me to his brother's home the next evening for a game of cards.

And there it happened. She was a pretty girl and her name was Clare. I just had to keep looking at her, and played my cards badly as a result.

They would not ask me again I was sure, but my host was an understanding man, and observant too. During supper I found myself sitting next to Clare, and my interest in her deepened. She was as good to talk to as she was to look at, and I had a sure feeling that she liked me.

She told me her evenings were nearly all taken up with Civil Defence work, but always each week she spent one evening with our mutual friend. I was more than delighted when I was invited to come along on the same evening.

My time in London was running short, and if I wished to know her better I had to act quickly. When we met again I asked her to let me take her out, and this was arranged for the next evening. She filled all my thoughts, and in that short time, I knew she was the one person I had been looking for.

The next night was one of London's worst experiences. I had difficulty in making my way towards Clare's home, where I had arranged to meet her. The bus I travelled in was forced to make a diversion due to an "incident" on its normal route, and I was set down in unfamiliar surroundings.

When I eventually reached the road where Clare lived I was almost an hour late for my appointment. And then I saw ahead of me a crowd; police, Civil Defence workers, and all that went with them on these occasions. As I reached the spot I realised that the house I was looking for was now no more than a heap of rubble.

In the next few hours I tried to find out what had happened to Clare, by my efforts were futile. The next day I was recalled from leave, and in a very short time was on my way overseas. I wrote several letters to Clare at her home address, hoping they would be forwarded to her. But I never received a reply.

Upon being invalided home, I returned to London and wandered round the places I had known before. Then one day I sat in a park some distance from Clare's former home.

Along the path came a girl. I knew even at a distance that it was she. As she came towards me I half rose from my seat and opened my mouth to speak; she turned her head in my direction, her eyes on my face - then she walked on without the least sign of recognition.

She had cut me dead.

I hadn't the heart to do anything about it. I went home and resumed my civilian occupation. A couple of years later I again met the fellow who had been responsible for introducing me to Clare. It was some time, however, before I plucked up sufficient courage to ask about her.

He told me: "She was married twelve months ago. To a very good chap who will look after her well. She manages very well, but I don't think she will ever get over it."

I looked at him, puzzled.

Then he said; "When her home was destroyed she suffered an injury which took away her sight." She has been blind since that awful night, and will never see again.

Padraig Na Riann - Ward 1A

December 1948 Vol VII No 11

HANDS' SERVICE

Hands on the coverlet, slender and white,
Nails shaped and polished, a dream of delight
Yet what have they done in life's greatest fight -
In duty and service to others?

See that old lady in bed over there -
Look at her hands quietly folded in prayer,
Can you not see how they're toil-worn with care,
Through a life-time of service to others?

A nurse's hands must always be near,
Swift, kindly, patient, to soothe away fear,
Day in, day out; year after year,
Doing worthwhile service to others.

Here is the doctor with hands sure and strong,
Treating his patients who suffer so long,
Efficient and ready when things all go wrong -
What a wonderful way to serve others.

Slim hands, plump hands, large hands and small,
Old folk, young folk, the short and the tall,
God has a job he can find for them all -
Seeking voluntary service to others.

B. Mangan, Ward 1A

December 1948 Vol VII No. 11

THE VISIT OF MANCHESTER UNITED

On the evening of 1st October 1948, the patients at Baguley Sanatorium were visited by some personalities who hit the headlines in the soccer world last season. There were the Cup-holders - Manchester United.

Complete with the F.A. Cup and Cup-winners' medals, they came in full force: Crompton, Carey, Aston, Anderson, Chilton, Cockburn, Delaney, Morris, Rowley, Pearson, Mitten, trainer, Mr Murphy, club secretary, Mr Crickmer and the ex-Manchester City, Liverpool and Scottish International, Matt Busby ...... men whose names are as familiar to football fans as those of their next door neighbours.

The called first of all at the male patients' Day Room, where they were welcomed by the Medical Superintendent, Dr Trayer, and a crowd of excited enthusiasts. The Cup was placed on a table, in a prominent position for all to see and the players settled down to receive an address of welcome from Dr Trayer, to which Matt Busby replied. He explained that they had received thousands of invitations and requests to visit various people. Experience had taught him that the best method of sorting out these many invitations was to put it to the players themselves for their opinions. This he had done with the letter from Baguley Sanatorium. The players had been unanimous in their decision to come and visit us at their first opportunity. They hoped they would win the Cup again and if successful would pay us another visit.

The players then brought out their medals and passed them round, the patients seeking out their own particular favourite, and many questions and opinions were discussed. I asked Jack Rowley whom he considered the best centre half he had played against and he replied without any hesitation, "Stan Cullis of Wolverhampton Wanderers, and the best two inside forwards, 'Raich' Carter and Wilf Mannion." After some time in the Day Room the players left, to visit the bed patients. Ward 5 was the first, then Ward 3. This was no formal "walk through." The players broke up into small groups and went to the beds of the patients for a chat, to sign autographs and pass their medals round, whilst the Cup was lifted on to the bed of anyone who wanted to examine it. Leaving Ward 3 they passed on to Ward 6A. here every cubicle was visited and many amusing incidents occurred. The Sister of the Ward, wishing to have the autographs of the players, but not having any notepaper, had all their names written on the hem of her white apron. Then there was the patient who had a photograph of Manchester City on the end of his bed. Jack Rowley, with a grin on his face, brought his famous left foot into play and made a playful kick at it. I hate to think what would have happened to that photograph if he had connected.

From 6A, the team crossed over the female patients' wards, 1A and 1B. Most of the players going on ahead, I followed with Chilton, Rowley, Cockburn and Delaney. When we arrived at the Day Room on 1A, the welcome had to be seen to be believed. The players were jammed tight, cheerfully signing autographs as fast as they could. I got inside the door, then quickly stepped back with a body swerve that would have done credit to Matt Busby himself. Eventually, all the ladies were satisfied that they had got all the autographs of the visitors, who then left, obviously very impressed by the reception they had received from everyone.

Summing up, here are a few impressions that I shall always remember: First of all Matt Busby, continually chewing gum and strolling among his players with the air of a happy father watching his boys at play. The bubbling enthusiasm of the impish Henry Cockburn, who did a mock dribble up the main drive with an imaginary ball. A delight to watch!

Unassuming Johnny Carey, the captain, who always seemed to be missing when anyone wanted him.

The look of bewilderment on Stan Pearson's face, finding he had exhausted two fountain pens signing autographs and having to use mine.

Yes! A great night!

To the three ladies who asked me for my autograph, I would say it was an honour indeed, but I am afraid they would have taken a very poor view on reading in their autograph books: E Manwaring 6A.

In conclusion I would just like to say ...... Thanks, Manchester United. Thanks a lot! Good Luck and Good Shooting.

E Manwaring, 6A.

June 1949 Vol. VIII No. 1

THE DEBT WE OWE

In war he was a hero,
One of the gallant few.
High above our island home,
On constant guard, he flew,
Performing feats of valour
Against our mortal foe.
Though mem'ries of the conflict dim
Let's not forget - the debt we owe.

In war he was a hero,
Fighting on foreign soil.
Grumbling maybe, now and then,
In action - always loyal.
Proving that our island blood
Could more than match the foe.
Now that the hour of trial has passed
Let's not forget - the debt we owe.

In war he was a hero,
Sailing the hazardous seas.
Keeping those who threatened us
To Davy Jones below.
But now the seas are safe again
Let's not forget - the debt we owe.

Though we'll not forget those men
Who died for Britain's cause,
What of those who came back home
From out Death's gaping jaws?
Surely now it's up to us
In every way to show,
That they are not forgotten men
And remember - the debt we owe.

J W Midson, Ward 6A

December 1949 Vol. VIII No. 3

THE PATIENTS PLEA

Spending weeks in bed becomes a tedious affair,
And after months and months, it seems impossible to bear,
The Doctor comes round every day, walks in and says "Hello,"
You lie their hoping for "Bed One" but once again it's "No."
Perhaps tomorrow he will bring the news you're waiting for,
It's whispered round, "The Doctor's here," the patients' hopes all soar.
You wonder if the day will bring the words you long to hear.
The pulses quicken hopefully, the Doctor's drawing near.
But all he says is "No 'Bed One' your temperature's too high,
Four hours of 'Flat Rest' every day is what you'll have to try."
The next one waits, with baited breath, declaring she is fine,
Out comes the Doctor's pen, which is an optimist sign.
He hesitates, and scans the chart, you wonder what he'll do,
Then with a twinkle in his eye, says, "Two more hours for you."
Can this be true? At last you've got what you've been waiting for,
But in another week or two you start expecting more.
The Doctor's sympathetic, and he understands your aim,
The biggest thrill is when he says "Your X-ray's turned out fine
You're going home on Thursday, though it's been a long, long time";
So don't despair you "Absolutes" who see no hours in view,
The day will come when you will hear the same thing said to you.
However long it may seem now, you too with reach the bend,
And like the rest of us, your stay will also find an end.

Camille Ades, Ward 1A

March 1950 Vol. VIII No. 4

SUMMER HOLIDAY

I planned my summer holiday,
And planned it well ahead.
I studied all the guide books,
And swiftly my thoughts sped.

> Switzerland: scenes of alpine glory,
> New York: a sky-scraper's top storey.
> Paris: beautiful in the spring
> (Or so the crooners often sing).

> Scots history always appealed to me,
> As did the charm of a silvery sea.
> A country cottage can steal my heart,
> Oh! how I've travelled from the start.

> I came to the conclusion
> I'd cross the Irish Sea,
> To the land of wit and blarney,
> T'was just the place for me.

I planned my summer holiday,
And planned it well ahead.
Little did I think to spend it
In a Baguley bed.

                              Anon, Ward 1B.

TAKING "THE CURE" IN DAVOS

The great day draws near for the lucky few who have been selected by their Regional Hospital Boards for treatment in a Swiss sanatorium under the National Health Scheme. They are lucky, because, in the first place, they are suitable cases - six months medical treatment is all that is considered necessary to do the trick, and, secondly, there are only 130 beds for all England and Wales - eighty male and fifty female.

Perhaps they have had to wait a few months in an English sanatorium, and now they are excited, perhaps a little apprehensive at the prospect of being so far from their relatives and friends. A Red Cross official has been to see them and advised them about clothing and money, and told them they can have a parcel sent duty free once a month.

What will it be like? How will they travel? Is it very different from the English sanatorium to which they have been accustomed?

They travel from various sanatoria in the provinces to a reception unit at New Cross Hospital, London, where they rest for two days and become acquainted with the other men and women with whom they will make the journey.

A coach takes them to *Folkestone*, stopping in a country lane on the way there whilst they eat the lunch which was packed for them at New Cross Hospital.

At *Calais*, there is a bewildering rush of porters and customs officials, and before they realise what is happening, they find themselves in a special carriage attached to the Basle train, and the French Red Cross people presenting them with a hot meal. Soon they settle down for the night in sleeping compartments. The train rumbles on through France, and they wake up at 6 a.m. to find themselves in *Basle*.

Yes, this really is Switzerland. Everywhere is covered with snow. On through the lowlands, past wooden chalets and lakes to *Zurich*. More and more mountains appear, like pillars of salt.

Recreation Hall and Chapel

Nurses recreation room

Stage in Recreation Hall and Chapel

At Landquart they change to a little mountain railway. It is like a scenic railway through Fairyland - glistening snow, Christmas trees, breathtaking mountains, and from everything hang icicles, giving that extra touch of magic. Tired but enthralled, they arrive at *Davos*, twenty eight-hours after leaving London. Here they are met by another contingent of Red Cross; the men are taken to the Angleterre Sanatorium and the women to the Park Sanatorium.

Their first impression is that of an hotel rather than a hospital. Two patients share a room and balcony. The nursing staff consists of a few Swiss and German sisters, who give such treatment as injections and chart temperatures.

For the first few days, the patients are confined to their rooms, whilst all the usual investigations are carried out - medical examinations, X-rays, blood and sputum tests. Then a course of treatment is decided upon.

There is no absolute bed rest as in an English sanatorium, *all* patients being allowed up for toilet. First grading is bed on the balcony, with all meals served on a tray. Next grade is a balcony chair, with a fleecy lined sleeping bag and blankets. Eventually the patient is allowed downstairs for meals, when they are then classed as "up" patients. If progressing satisfactorily, a morning walk, then an afternoon walk is allowed.

Rest periods are much longer than in England and even when on maximum activity, each patient is compelled to observe strictly to the following: -

1.	9.15 a.m. to 11 a.m.	}	Reading and talking are allowed, but
2.	12 noon to 1 p.m.	}	writing or occupational therapy.
3.	2 p.m. to 4 p.m.	}	Absolute rest. No talking, reading etc.
4.	5.30 p.m. to 6.30 p.m.	}	As in the morning.

Walks, if allowed, are taken between 11 a.m. and noon, and 4.30 p.m. and 5.30 p.m.

Medical treatment is similar to that in England. Chemotherapy - P.A.S., streptomycin, rimifom etc. Artificial pneumothorax may be induced, and adhesions divided, but no major operations are performed in either National Health sanatoriums owing to the high cost of surgery in Switzerland.

There is an English doctor appointed by the Ministry of Health to act as liaison between the patients and Swiss doctors. Two members of the British Red Cross society are also resident in Davos, to attend to patients' welfare, and advise when social problems arise.

Both the Angleterre and Park sanatoria have a committee of up-patients to organise entertainments. There is the usual chairman, secretary and treasurer, with other members of the committee to look after a shop, library, emergency Red Cross clothing, the ordering and delivering of English newspapers.

There is a film show once a week, a coach taking the patients from one sanatorium to the other, according to where it is held. Up patients are usually allowed out to see any big winter sports events, such as the World Skating Championships (which were given a lot of publicity in the English newspapers), and ski-jumping competitions.

In April and May the snow melts and everywhere is a riot of colour with the alpine spring flowers. Then, perhaps, the lucky up-patients are allowed occasional outings - a coach trip to Leichtenstein, St. Moritz or the Matterhorn.

It must be stressed that these activities are only allowed if the patient's medical condition permits. Most, and sometimes all, their time is spent resting on the balcony.

All around them are the dazzling white Alps; the woods where they take their walks; the squirrels, the birds and the wild deer. They can see the skiers on the slopes and hear and see sports in which they can take no part.

Yes. They are very lucky and grateful to have such a wonderful opportunity and only wish more patients were able to enjoy treatment in Switzerland. But ask any of them what they think about most all.

It is the return journey, down the mountains to Landquart, to Zurich, Basle and Calais, their first glimpse of England - the white cliffs of Dover and HOME.

The San Toy continued until the Summer Edition - July 1954, when Dr Hugh G Trayer said goodbye. The Editor's Postscript read:

*"It is all over, bar the shouting. You have read the contents and you have probably found this edition of San Toy lacking in many things. But one thing it does not lack. And that is the warmth of the affection, gratitude and respect in which we hold Doctor Trayer. I should like to thank the Lord Mayor of Manchester, Alderman R S Harper, for his willingness and kindness in providing a 'lead' for this edition of San Toy. I should like also th thank the contributors, both inside and outside the Sanatorium. On the cover appears the words "Last Edition". I don't know whether they are prophetic. But if this is the last edition - **San Toy** is nearly twenty years old - then this magazine had done the job it set out to do. If not, then we can look forward to bigger and better editions of **San Toy** in the years to come.*

The Editor.

The San Toy ceased publication due to the lack of contributions and the difficulty in finding suitable editorial staff. It had, over the years, fulfiled and encouraged the community spirit that was so important in Baguley Sanatorium at that time. Thanks are due to all who contributed to its success, wherever they may be.

The cover of the very last San Toy magazine produced in July 1954